JUST THE

FINANCIAL

FACTS

JUST THE

FINANCIAL

FACTS

How to Identify
Nuggets of Usable
News and Minimize
Information
Overload

Michael C. Thomsett

DEARBORN™
T R A D E
A **Kaplan Professional** Company

Vice President and Publisher: Cynthia A. Zigmund
Senior Managing Editor: Jack Kiburz
Interior Design: Lucy Jenkins
Cover Design: Design Solutions
Cover Illustration: Tim Lee/SIS
Typesetting: Elizabeth Pitts

Published by Dearborn Trade, a Kaplan Professional Company

Printed in the United States of America

01 02 03 10 9 8 7 6 5 4 3 2 1

Library of Congress Cataloging-in-Publication Data

Thomsett, Michael C.
    Just the financial facts : how to identify nuggets of usable news
and minimize information overload / Michael C. Thomsett.
        p.   cm.
    Includes index.
    ISBN 0-7931-4368-3 (pbk.)
    1. Investments—Information services.   I. Title.
HG4515.9 .T482   2001
332.63'2042—dc21

                                            2001000292

Dearborn Trade books are available at special quantity discounts to use for sales promotions, employee premiums, or educational purposes. Please call our Special Sales Department to order or for more information, at 800-621-9621, ext. 4364, or write Dearborn Trade Publishing, 155 N. Wacker Drive, Chicago, IL 60606-1719.

CONTENTS

PREFACE
What This Book Will Do for You   vii

INTRODUCTION
Facts and Figures–and More Figures   ix

1. Financial News   1

2. Finding Your Own Hidden Nuggets   25

3. Stock Market Listings   40

4. Bond Market Listings   71

5. Mutual Fund Listings   92

6. Derivatives: Options and Futures   113

7. Technical Indicators   145

8. Fundamental Indicators   164

9. Economic Indicators   192

INDEX   211

What This Book Will Do for You

Intuition becomes increasingly valuable in the new information society precisely because there is so much data.

—John Naisbitt and Patricia Aburdene (*Re-inventing the Corporation*, 1985)

Information. It is so abundant and available, but we all have difficulty managing it. Effective investors are forced to determine which pieces of information are valuable and which are not helpful in making the important decisions about their portfolios.

The financial press provides the raw data for investors. At the very least, information on a Web page or in a newspaper can be absorbed within a finite period of time. This is comforting, because each investor knows that all other investors are sharing in the same sources of information. That levels the playing field—or does it? Perhaps the more intuitive investors are able to interpret the financial news with greater skill than the average person, because they understand what the news really reveals or does not reveal.

This book is intended to provide insights into how the financial news can help you to make informed decisions about your investments. Because investors are analytical by nature, financial news is easily digested. The majority of investors find comfort in having numbers and reported trends, indexes, averages, and percentages presented—in columns of numbers and in graphs. Progress is measured easily, because it is based on current reporting and regular updates. Readers of the financial press believe that they are getting reliable information that enables them to stay on top of a changing market. However, with so much news in papers and on the Internet, are investors really being well served? Does the information in the press provide interpretive news, or is it simply the raw material? Every investor needs to determine the answer to this question in order to make informed decisions. In fact, the basic information provided in the financial press does not answer investors' questions. It is only the raw material, the basic information that needs to be interpreted.

This fact is critical for investors, because it is not the accumulation of information that makes investors successful; rather, it is the skillful interpretation and application of information. This book is intended to provide guidelines for using the financial news to manage individual portfolios and identify changes in the fundamental and technical strength of a company that may lead investors to make informed decisions. These decisions are not based on information alone, but on knowledge about how to translate raw data into valuable market insight.

Facts and Figures– and More Figures

Investors *want* to believe. Always looking for a better way,
a chance to gain an advantage in the market, they are
particularly susceptible to arguments that use statistics.

   –Mark A. Johnson (*The Random Walk and Beyond,* 1988)

Have you ever thought that there is too much information available about the market? You already know that a big problem is deciding which forms of information to use and which to ignore. The financial press provides investors with a wealth of basic information, but it is up to each individual to take that raw material and interpret it.

The typical financial newspaper lists dozens of potential markets–stocks, bonds, mutual funds, options, futures, foreign exchange, and more. You also can read about valuation in numerous domestic and international exchanges. This is further supplemented by thousands of online sites, each offering valuable information that "everyone" must have. Not only would you have to be an expert economist to interpret all of this raw material, you also would need to be an accountant to understand all of the financial information and news thrown your way. It's a problem for every investor, and all too often the response–born in frustration–is to seek a simple solution, a single, easily understood method for making decisions that does not require a lot of analysis, compilation, or interpretation. Unfortunately, this approach often misleads investors rather than providing useful methods for managing their money.

This book is based on the premise that information in financial newspapers and magazines, published through subscription services or available online, represents a vast array of raw data; that some of that raw data is valuable in helping you to mold a decision-making process; and that you need to interpret the information to suit your own requirements. A popular error is to believe that the financial press provides answers; this idea is fostered by the financial press itself, because sellers of information recognize that people want answers. However, what you really get in the press is opinions, interpretations of information. Financial news should not be considered as advice or recommendation, because it is not tailored to your own portfolio.

Taking financial news as advice is the same as hearing rumor and believing it to be factual without investigating on your own. (This happens frequently in the Wall Street world.) An astute observer knows that rumor cannot be used reliably for making decisions involving putting money at risk. Financial news is a presentation of a broad array of facts, without any real interpretation. It is perhaps a disservice to investors that some news sources have taken it on themselves to attempt to tell investors what the news means. But this is the nature of journalism. Although journalism originated with the gathering and presenting of facts, modern news providers believe that their job is to tell readers what the news means and how they should react to it. They appeal to the herd mentality that we often see on Wall Street as a whole. Listening to journalists and market analysts and then acting on their advice is a mistake. *The real expert on your portfolio is you.* Only you know your level of risk tolerance, your personal goals and strategies, and the lengths to which you are able and willing to go to achieve your goals.

This book presents detailed explanations of each of the different types of financial listings and analyses and explains what the information reveals. Ironically, the most basic information often is misunderstood even by long-term investors. So the approach in the early chapters is to pick apart the details of each type of listing, explain what it shows, and then provide ideas about how you can take that information, interpret it, and give it meaning. In this way, you will be able to identify indicators that help you to develop your own opinions rather than rely on the opinions of others. You will be able to use the news in a way that makes the most sense.

In the latter part of the book, chapters are concerned with examining what is reported in the press beyond the daily or weekly listings. Technical, fundamental, and economic indicators and news, plus periodic reports about listed companies have significant value to investors. However, many individuals find themselves in a quandary. They read a news story about a company whose stock they own, and they understand what the story reports. But they really know neither how to take such news to the next step—using that information to understand how it affects or changes the value of the stock as an investment—nor what it means in terms of potential future value.

Let's say you own 300 shares in XYZ Corporation, and you read in a major financial newspaper the following story:

The board of XYZ Corporation announced this morning the approval by the FDA of their long-awaited drug for the treatment of many cancers. However, the board added, the products will not be available to the public until resolution of pending litigation concerning safety of the new drugs. The suit, now pending in New Jersey's court system, alleges that the drug's tests were not performed in a reliable manner, and that the drug poses a threat to health. The board cited FDA approval as supporting their position that the drug is ready for human use, but they predicted that no sales are likely to occur for at least two more years.

This fictitious story may have ramifications for investors. For example, were analysts expecting the drug to be available this year? Will this latest news adversely affect the stock's market value? Is there a chance that the drug will never be approved? These troubling questions are implied in the story, and each investor needs to be able to determine the answer to the salient question: *How does this news affect the value of my investment?*

It is a reasonably straightforward matter to look at news and information and accept it at face value. However, it is the contention throughout this book that all investors will benefit by going beyond the news and, at the very least, identifying how and why information affects their investment portfolio. If you are considering buying shares of stock, current news and valuation certainly should be used in making your decision. If you own shares of stock, you need to monitor the company as well as the market value of your investment in order to determine whether continuing to hold those shares makes sense.

In the market, most of the emphasis is placed on the presentation of news in a broad format and little is placed on the analysis of individual stocks. Investors tend to be preoccupied with movement of market averages and indexes, overall trading volume, and mood barometers. Unfortunately, none of these broad indicators helps you in the management of your individual stocks. They may be useful in deciding whether to invest in the market in one respect: markets are cyclical and if you decide that the timing is poor for investing in common stocks, your decision certainly may be based on overall indicators. However, individuals who own shares of stock directly tend to have a few well-selected stocks and often intend to hold those shares as long-term investments. In this instance, momentary indicators of larger market mood are not revealing, nor do they help investors to decide whether to stay in the market or get out.

Many popular indicators share this problem. They reveal something about the market on average, but they provide no information that is useful to you. Overall averages are like composite weather reports. If the weather report on the evening news told you only that the average daily high temperature in North America was 67 degrees today, what value would that have for you? If the meteorologist further reports that this represents an overall warming trend, does it help you to decide whether to wear a jacket outdoors? Of course not. But in the stock market, this is the nature of the information that you receive in terms of overall markets. It is interesting in some ways, but it is of no help in the management of the handful of stocks and shares of mutual funds in your portfolio.

This book will reveal how information is presented, which forms of information are useful and which are merely distracting, and how to take a small portion of news and information and apply it to make informed decisions. Just as your local weather forecast helps you decide what to wear tomorrow or whether to plan a picnic, the individualized study of a company's market strength helps you decide whether its stock is a good fit for your portfolio.

CHAPTER **1**

Financial News

Information is the equalizer; it breaks down the hierarchy. A lot of institutions are living in a world that is rapidly passing them by.

–Edmund G. Brown Jr. (*Esquire*, February 1978)

Unwary investors might not know when they are reading real news or when the information being provided is thinly disguised advertising. This is the nature of financial news. The "spin" on what is happening in the market or to a particular company does more to distort information than to actually inform.

This is not to say that no good information can be gained from the various sources—newspapers, magazines, subscriptions services, annual reports, and so on—but only to point out that the informed investor needs to develop a critical eye when reading stories in the financial media.

NEWS VERSUS INFORMATION

When is it just news, and when is it actual information? Or do the two words mean the same thing? Remember that the news is a genre of publishing whose purpose is to get and keep the reader's interest, usually in an easily comprehended and highly abbreviated form. That means that a particular angle needs to be put on otherwise dry information. News often requires that the raw data of information be taken and formed into a story of great interest to the reader. The journalist seeks the brief, easy way to convey information, but that is not always a good way to present the complexities of the market. As a consequence, the financial news tends to oversimplify even the most complex issues.

> **KEY POINT:** Remember that the journalist's task is to hold your attention. That means putting an interesting angle on the story, but not necessarily the most informative one.

Consider the following examples of how raw data can be transformed into an interesting story:

Raw data—Trianameta, a company that has been publicly listed for less than one year, reported earnings of 4 percent for the quarter, in line with what was forecast. Higher sales are forecast for the coming six months. Trianameta's management said it is pleased with the results, as the company is competing with larger, better-established firms in the same field.

Interesting story—Maverick go-getter beats start-up odds: Trianameta, a gutsy new start-up and last year's big surprise, took on the competition last quarter, turning out a 4 percent net profit. In spite of some analysts' pessimism, Trianameta predicts even more for the next two quarters, proving that it's still possible to beat the odds.

Another example involving financial reporting:

Raw data—Encomar Pharmaceuticals has announced a dividend of 55 cents per share, to be paid on September 5 to shareholders of record as of August 21. This is the third straight increase in quarterly dividends for Encomar. Spokespersons said that Encomar intends to continue modest increases for the coming year. Management pointed to consistent growth in quarterly profits as justification for the decision to increase dividend payments.

Interesting story–Dividends surge for small Rx stock: For the third straight quarter, Encomar has raised its quarterly dividend, pleasing stockholders and surprising analysts. Trying to keep the good news coming, the company plans even more increases in the future. Ex-dividend is August 21, and payment of 55 cents per share is scheduled for September 5. Encomar is the rising star in the pharmaceuticals sector, reporting profits every quarter, and one of the new favorites on the growth track among companies listed for five years or less.

Neither of the interesting stories distorts or changes the information, but each places a different angle on the raw data so that readers will be informed *and* entertained. It's a matter of making the information interesting, but there is a thin line between giving information some appeal and telling the reader what to think about the report. Because that line is difficult to identify, it creates a constant problem for journalists. Some journalism involves editorial comment or opinion even when it is not intended.

There is a tendency in the financial media not only to make stories interesting, but also to emphasize the extremes. So good news becomes very good news, and bad news becomes dire. This makes reports more interesting to read while they also report the facts. In some cases, news that is neutral is distorted to make a story more interesting for the reader. Unfortunately, editorial pressure often causes journalists to emphasize the entertainment value of the story, and the facts may be buried or even left out.

Dry financial information has to be simplified, shortened, and explained for quick communication; this often is not possible without some distortion. Another difficulty is that the distinction between news and editorial is a difficult one. However, the major financial papers do a good job of keeping the two separate: for the most part, the financial print media are sophisticated, use reliable information sources, and report the news honestly.

> **KEY POINT:** It is the nature of journalism to simplify the facts and report in extremes. Reporters are aware that a reader's attention span is short, which means that financial reporting tends to stress the high and low points, with little in the way of in-depth analysis.

There are alternatives to getting information via the financial press. Online news sources, which are far more plentiful than print sources, tend to treat financial news as one more section within a broader base of reporting, and generally have less depth or analysis. Subscription services that offer financial and technical information, such as Value Line and Standard & Poor's, provide reliable, high-quality information. Annual reports issued by companies tend to be the least reliable sources for information; although their numbers are audited independently, the annual report is a public relations document intended to attract and keep shareholders and to put the best possible spin on news about the company. Anyone who has read an annual report knows that it is rare to see any kind of negative spin put on bad news about the company. If the document speaks about a disappointing result, it usually is placed in the context of a promise of better times to come. Annual reports define the future as "that period of time in which our affairs prosper, our friends are true and our happiness is assured."*

Remember that one of management's primary tasks is to ensure that the price of corporate stock grows. The informa-

---

*Ambrose Bierce, *The Devil's Dictionary,* 1906.

tion provided in the annual report may be accurate, but it is placed in the best possible light. Messages from the president or CEO are written by public relations departments or consultants. Their purpose is to express the most promising possible angle on the year's results. An example:

How the numbers came out—Sales were down by 30 percent from previous years, and profits were off 42 percent. A long labor strike and a class-action lawsuit prevented the company from expanding as it had planned, and a new lawsuit was filed one month before the annual report was issued.

Reporting the news—This was a year of consolidation for the company. We experienced reduced sales volume due to labor contract discussions, but management believes that its discourse with the two major unions has yielded not only new contracts, but also a more solid and productive bond between management and labor. We are working together to ensure prosperity in coming years, and the short-lived slowdown of last year is behind us. The decline in profits is a rebuilding opportunity. The legal issues that characterize the past year will not deter us from planned expansion in four areas: product development, geographic growth, quality-assurance programs, and improved capitalization. To these ends, management is negotiating in many arenas to continue the theme of growth in coming years.

Another example:

How the numbers came out—During the past year, analysts predicted that profits would increase from the 7 percent of sales previously reported, to 8 percent for the year. Instead, profits were at 7 percent once again, disappointing the market and resulting in a falling price for the stock.

Reporting the news—This year demonstrated management's consistency in producing a good return on sales. The 7 percent yield enabled us to continue the long-established program for dependability and long-term financial strength. In the fourth quarter, management announced that the company will continue to buy its own stock and to retire it as long as the market price remains at current levels. We anticipate continued consistent returns on sales and expansion of our markets, not only in the coming year, but far into the future as well.

These examples demonstrate how annual reports can make disappointing or mundane news both interesting and optimistic without changing the facts. It is the job of the public relations department employee to make any news good news. Consider the role of the public relations department in the reporting of dry product development news:

The basic information—PlyTech has developed a new lens that improves the ability of medical researchers to analyze cell changes at the molecular level. This latest advance results from over five years of research and combines several technologies used in cancer research.

The news report—High-tech lab announces revolutionary new cancer research tool: PlyTech, developers of medical instruments, announced the release of a dynamic, state-of-the-art lens this week. The new lens competes well with less-efficient technology in medical research instrumentation. The new lens, the outcome of a five-year development project, continues the innovative approach to science for which PlyTech is known. "We can't cure cancer yet," says Gunther Weller, project engineer with PlyTech, "but this is yet another step toward that end."

It is worth developing the skill of spotting the differences between objective reporting and public relations spin on the news. Just as you need to be aware of the differences between news and opinion in the newspaper, you must also make a distinction between raw data and spin.

KEY POINT: The usefulness of financial news is in the raw data it supplies to you. But avoid the mistake of taking raw data as conclusive information.

THE VALIDITY OF INDEX REPORTING IN THE MEDIA

The dominant theme in media reports on the market is an obsession with index reporting. For some investors, the index is the market. When they track movement in the Dow Jones Industrial Average (DJIA), the S&P 500, or some other index, they believe that they are following the market.

The truth is that the DJIA is not a representative index. Changes in the DJIA certainly affect overall stock volume and price change, but the market comprises thousands of stocks and not just the 30 that are tracked through the DJIA. The S&P 500 is a far more representative test of market activity and is often cited for comparisons of rates or return, but it doesn't represent all the companies in the market. Still, market reports are presented as though indexes were the entire market.

This tendency reflects a prevailing mood of optimism. Consider the choice of language about changes in the DJIA, both in the press and in other media:

- *Rising market*–The Dow surged today on reports of higher earnings.
- *Falling market*–Prices reacted to profit-taking this morning.
- *Rising market*–Renewed optimism helped the market to come back strongly.
- *Falling market*–Prices retreated slightly due to consolidation.

How valid is the media's reporting of indexes? Does the daily or weekly change in market indexes help you to become a more informed investor? Index watching can help you to judge the mood of the market because the index is a reflection of that mood to some degree, although no index can be thought of as a conclusive and far-reaching measurement of market mood. If you do believe in watching the overall market, you also need to assess the overall mood in terms of how it affects your portfolio. If the fundamentals of your stocks are solid, then weekly or monthly changes in the DJIA will have no long-term effect on your profitability. If your stocks react strongly to market volatility, your greater concern should be for long-term growth prospects of the companies whose stock you own.

> **KEY POINT:** Even though the media place a lot of emphasis on indexes and averages, most investors want more basic information about their stocks. Am I making money or losing it? Should I sell? Should I buy more shares?

One reason to discount the value of index reporting is that institutional holdings account for a large portion of volume on the market. Large firms, notably mutual funds, invest heavily in the stocks included in the DJIA, so decisions by mutual funds to buy or sell stock often have significant impact on the index—even if individuals, or "retail" investors, have opposing sentiments about the stocks involved.

It is no easy task to judge the overall market. At the very least, you need to analyze the news for each company on an individual basis, and not be pulled in to the populist methods of reporting market strength or weakness as measured by an index.

COMPARATIVE PROFIT REPORTING

One of the more useful forms of information available in the financial media is the articles that appear from time to time about specific companies. The financial media index stories by company and provide readers with easy reference to the page numbers where stories of immediate interest appear. The *Wall Street Journal* calls theirs the "Index to Businesses." In *Barron's,* it is called "Index to Companies." And *Investor's Business Daily* provides readers with a one-page summary of "Business News" in its first section.

Financial news in all three papers tends to combine analysis, announcement, and forecasting in a mix of stories by company or sector, or on a market-wide basis. Ever-present predictions about upcoming rallies or new records on the indexes are mixed with pure news reports about antitrust matters, labor negotiations, earnings, management announcements, mergers, strikes, and more.

Within the stories, emphasis is placed upon comparison. A company's current-year sales and profits, according to the financial journalists, are supposed to exceed last year's. If a company's sales and profits level out or fall, it is bad news, and it is reported as such. This aspect of financial reporting is like the tracking of sports records—we expect the team or company to break its own record and to do better than the competition.

KEY POINT: To really understand how the financial news is reported, compare the financial pages to the sports pages.

Expecting improvement year after year is far from realistic. The accounting norms for reporting sales and profits recognize that there is a natural limit to all financial outcomes. Sales will not increase forever, and the yield on sales is likewise limited, for good reason. A company cannot continually increase the markup on its products or services so that profits continue to grow, because its competitors will take away its market share. Companies are competing with one another constantly, and they have to balance the desire for growth and profits against competitive forces. In an industry where an 8 percent profit is the norm, it should be enough that a corporation maximizes its efforts and earns 8 percent year after year. In a sector with many strong competitors, every market will be finite; there are only enough customers to go around, so it is not practical to expect a company's sales and profits to grow each and every year.

The real tests of corporate success are customer service, the quality of the products or services being sold, the quality of management, and—especially where the market is concerned—the price of the stock. Another important feature is the consistency of returns, which translates to dependability in the market. This fundamental-volatility test determines how consistent a corporation's reported sales and profits are. There is no real problem with consistent results or with slow growth. In many cases, lack of growth is the more desirable outcome. Expansion for its own sake can have a detrimental effect on customer service, quality, and profit. Uncontrolled expansion may create losses because costs and expenses are not monitored in an ever-changing corporate environment. Intelligent corporate managers recognize the need for slow, steady growth when it is justified; they also know that expansion is not always a positive experience. Management needs to maintain the ability to produce profits consistently, so if sales are to expand, they need to expand in a controlled environment in which profits are consistent and the quality of products and services is not compromised.

It is a peculiar American myth, and one that is widely accepted, that a company has to continue to expand or it will go out of business. There is no sound rationale for this belief, and in fact, continual expansion may be the culprit for many business failures. For companies that have made it through the first year or two, the most common cause of subsequent failure is rapid and uncontrolled expansion—growing sales that are not necessarily accompanied by corresponding profits. Some inexperienced business managers believe that growth in sales always means increased profit margins. The real test of a company's quality should be its ability to maintain the same profit margin even when sales are rising. That is not always possible.

> **KEY POINT:** Expansion for its own sake can spell disaster. The myth that companies have to expand has no basis in fact. From a management point of view, uncontrolled expansion is one of the most significant threats to corporate strength.

The score-keeping approach to financial analysis, the test often applied by investors and almost always by journalists, is unsophisticated, but easy to understand; and that is the key. Journalists will look for the most interesting angle on a story, but not always the most important one. They will report information in the most easily understood, but not always the most accurate or realistic, manner. The reporting of corporate sales and profits is the prime example of this failure.

Can we expect better? Perhaps the investing public is so accustomed to the score-keeping approach to the market that it would not accept a more inquisitive or insightful media. Perhaps financial journalists are forced to report as they do because investors do not want to be bored with the more important but tedious aspects to a story. As an investor, you need to recognize that your money is at risk, so making decisions based on what is reported in the financial media might be a poor choice. You need to obtain more in-depth information than the interpretation of earnings reports.

It could be that sales at or below the previous year's level and profits at the same yield level mean corporate management is doing a stellar job. Resisting uncontrolled expansion can be difficult. Expansion is tempting, and if it is possible to grow, many a corporate manager will take the opportunity.

Only the most astute and talented corporate managers will ask the important questions:

- Is growth a wise course at this time?
- Can our internal systems and controls support growth?
- Do we have the built-in infrastructure to support growth without loss of quality?
- Can we change our systems so that we will maintain net yields?
- How can we control our rate of growth so that we do not lose control?

These are rather sophisticated concepts for the financial media to grasp or report. It is easier to convey an idea simply. Consider the following two examples of a corporate earnings story:

The analytical approach–thoughtful and cautious–that is the approach to growth adopted by management at Carso-Tech, Incorporated. The company has been listed publicly for only three years, and its profits have come in at 4.5 percent each year with regularity. "We attribute this to our resistance of uncontrolled growth," says CEO Mark Smith. "We want to grow slowly so that we do not jeopardize our position in the industry."

The company wants to ensure that its quality is not compromised by growth, so it is not aggressively seeking new contracts at this time. Smith explains: "If we are to expect to continue providing our products to the market, we cannot grow too quickly."

The usual approach–Slow growth reported for Carso-Tech–a disappointing 4.5 percent net was reported this week by CarsoTech, the new hi-tech company whose promising future was touted loudly two years ago. This yield, on stagnant sales of about the same level as the past two years, caused analysts to downgrade the company earlier this week.

CEO Mark Smith justified the poor results, claiming that the company did not want to grow too rapidly. However, in a field of competitors seeing 6 percent and 7 percent yields on sales growing by as much as 30 percent per year, investors question whether CarsoTech remains a viable long-term investment.

The second version of the story certainly is easier to understand. It also is far more interesting from a journalist's point of view. The comparison between years and between competitors is better "ink" than a thoughtful analysis of the value of expansion. In the competitive world of listed securities, the media are the primary interpreters of information. Investors develop their opinions on the basis of what they learn not from financial experts, but from financial reporters.

KEY POINT: Stories often emphasize the most interesting facts, but valid points can be lost in the process. This may translate to inaccuracy for the reader and injustice to the company that is the topic of the story.

LOOKING BEYOND THE REPORTED NEWS

The manner in which profits are reported is only the most visible symptom of the larger issue: the way that reporting takes place in general. Financial journalists face the challenge of putting the most appealing spin on what otherwise might be unacceptably dry stories. Unfortunately, journalists may put the wrong emphasis or spin on a financial article.

In the late 1990s, the federal government made substantial changes to the way it taxes residential home sales. The old rule was that profits could be deferred as long as the sale involved the primary residence and a new house was built or purchased within two years of the sale. Under the new law, primary residential sales are tax-free up to the first $500,000 of profit as long as the property was the primary residence for at least three of the previous five years. With this ruling, it became possible for the vast majority of homesellers to take profits out of their property without losing a substantial portion to income taxes. So a retiring couple could sell their home and earn as much as half a million dollars in profits with no federal tax liability. This was important tax relief also for young families trading one house for another or relocating in a different part of the country with vastly different property values.

For some time the financial media largely ignored the story, and when it was finally reported, the emphasis was completely wrong. Stories appeared about the new law that would finally make the rich pay their fair share of taxes: a rich person selling a home and earning $2 million in profit would be taxed on all profit above $500,000.

But clearly, the real story was that for the vast majority of people, the change provided real tax relief. Why did this distortion happen? Because it was more appealing in the journalistic sense to relate the story that way. The real story was lost in the more popular message: the rich now have to pay their share of taxes.

KEY POINT: The significance of a news story is quickly lost if the wrong point is emphasized. This is a chronic problem in the media in general. In the financial media, distortions can mislead investors into making expensive decisions.

This sort of treatment of stories is a great disservice to the public. When the basic facts are provided, the financial news has exceptionally good reporting. The daily rundown of financial information in the form of stock and other listings, dividend and earnings reports, and major corporate announcements, is excellent. It is timely and accurate, and it exposes financial readers to what is really going on. However, when journalists are left to put an angle on a story that enables them to take a soapbox for a favorite or popular political statement, they commit the worst form of distortion.

Several years ago, a story about tobacco stocks discussed the ongoing litigation against tobacco companies. The story began with an analysis of what would happen to tobacco stocks if states won their lawsuits against big tobacco. Then the story changed to a different angle; it became a medical story about the effects of smoking on women. The story included the amazing statistical statement that only half of all men had difficulty quitting smoking, whereas a full 50 percent of women had the same difficulty.

INFORMATION AND RUMOR

What is information and what is rumor? There is never a shortage of rumors about the market, and it is a wise policy for all investors to differentiate between fact and fiction (or unverified fact). Anyone who makes investment decisions solely on the basis of the word on the street is inviting trouble.

KEY POINT: Long-term investors should never make decisions under pressure. A good long-term opportunity will still be there tomorrow—in spite of what you hear to the contrary.

The wise investor is analytical and adopts the scientific approach to making investment decisions. That means that all information must be verified independently. Even a well-trusted indicator should never be used by itself as the basis for an investment decision. The idea that all indicators or news should be verified by a second source is a smart premise for investing. Speculators say that they must act quickly or miss an opportunity. While this might be desirable for speculators who are willing to take significant risks, it is not beneficial for long-term investors whose risk profile is vastly different.

With the financial media, as with the media in general, you cannot know how reliable news is at the time that you read it. Some time may need to pass before the initial story shakes out and the facts fall into place. The initial reports of major news events often are distorted, exaggerated, or downright incorrect. The same can be true of financial reports. It takes time for people to investigate the event, for knowledgeable participants to react to initial reports, and for journalists to sort out fact from rumor. Because journalists depend on their sources, the initial reports are not always reliable. So investors need to recognize financial journalism for what it is—the best information available at the time the paper went to press. Journalists also must meet their deadlines, another reason why information is always subject to later updates. This, added to the fact that reporters put angles on stories, makes it necessary to view financial reporting cautiously.

> **KEY POINT:** Use the financial news as your starting point. Develop reliable sources for more in-depth information, especially on the Internet, where access is not only instant, but also free.

When you read a story about a particular company, you might get a more informed version of the story by researching it further on your own. A review of financial reports might reveal more than the summarized report about sales and profits does. A letter or e-mail to the investor relations department of a company might provide a different angle on the story. A discussion with a stockbroker or fellow investor might be more revealing than the news story. So use your sources and investigate on your own. Use the financial media as primary sources for initial information, and then proceed with your own, more in-depth fact-finding mission. When it comes to the financial media, apply the old Russian proverb, *Doverey no proverey* ("Trust but verify").

In all fairness, the financial media are usually dependable sources for information. The raw data they provide is not only useful, but also essential for making informed investment decisions. However, it would be a mistake to allow the media reports of financial facts and figures to be the determining factor in your decision making. The news stories offer raw data only; you need to investigate further. Editorial information provided by the financial media, notably the weekly analysis in *Barron's,* offers a superior source for expert information in highly specialized areas like options or commodities. The writers of these editorials know their markets, and investors can learn a great deal by reading the opinions in all of the financial papers.

> **KEY POINT:** Editorial opinions in the financial media are exceptional sources of information. However, you need to make sure you know what you are reading. Is it news or opinion?

ONLINE SOURCES FOR NEWS

The Internet provides yet another source for information. As more investors are investing online, the usefulness of print newspapers begins to fade. This is not to say that the Internet will ever completely replace financial newspapers. But as more investors go online, more of them will get their information from news sources online as well.

It is important to make a distinction between two major sources of financial news on the Internet. If you are reading stories by generalized news sources, chances are that you will be getting the mainstream media's take on the news, which lacks the depth and quality you are more likely to find in news from a financial source. A general news reporter is qualified to write stories on a variety of topics without being an insider or expert. A financial reporter often is trained in finance and business; even though the angle might be questionable, the financial reporter's take on a story will be more informed than that of the more general news source.

> **KEY POINT:** If you get your information from a mainstream news source, you do not necessarily get the financial angle, just the general news angle.

In addition to being careful to distinguish between general news and financial news, you should avoid the pure rumor that is easy to find online and also avoid sales pitches disguised as news. Stay away from investment chat rooms. Not only are these poor sources for information, you also have no idea who is providing the information in them. Some Web sites offer online chats with experts in finance—corporate executives, brokers, authors, and others—and these are fine sources for focused information. However, the investment chat room where anyone who wants to can sign on and make statements is a dangerous source for information. The Internet is also full of advertising. Virtually every Web page has banners promising riches and secrets to wealth; don't click on these banners at all. As an investor, you should be looking for your information, not responding to advertising banners. Just as smart consumers do not respond to junk mail, smart investors do not believe what they read in Internet banners.

Here are some guidelines for selecting the best online sources for news and information:

1. Seek out a Web site with attractive overall design and graphics. It is easier to find information when a Web designer has put some thought into the appearance of the page and the arrangement of information.

2. Judge a page by how easy it is to find the links you want. When a page is designed with properly labeled links across the top or to the left, it makes your task easier, so

that you can go right to the page you need. (Placing links to the right is less practical, because viewers with smaller screens need to scroll over to find the extended area of the page.)

3. Is there a "contact us" link? You may need to get in touch with the sponsor of a site, and pages that display a contact link make this easy. Some Web sites have no contact link, or the link is buried somewhere and difficult to locate.

4. Prominent placement of the day's news stories is critical. Some sites place stories below advertising links or market news, so that you have to scroll down to find them. A well-designed site should place news stories in the middle of the top of the page so you can see them immediately.

5. A search feature that enables you to type in your word or phrase and look for it on the entire site saves time and effort. This practical feature is a big plus.

6. At-a-glance market statistics help you to perform a quick review without having to read through a lot of text. A well-designed site will provide you with quick summaries of the status of major indexes and markets. Graphics add to the value of this section.

7. A nicely designed site map is essential for navigating a Web site. You need to be able to select from a broad range of pages on the site without being barraged by promotional banners. Efficient site maps are a sign of thoughtful design.

8. Effective links to individual-portfolio tracking, stock quotes, and charts help you to use a site for more than financial news. Ultimately, a combination of ease of use and multiple applications define an exceptional Web site.

A Web site with any of the following three features will not be useful to you as an investor:

1. Pop-up promotional pages that are irritating and invasive. No one enjoys trying to find information on a Web site, only to have an uninvited new page appear suddenly. Avoid Web sites that employ pop-up advertising.
2. Avoid pages with prominent and excessive advertising banners, especially banners that appear above news and information or market updates. Placement of advertising before useful information tells you that the Web site's priorities are backward. You have to expect some advertising on all free Internet sites, but the best sites provide ads in a discreet manner.
3. Finally, stay away from Web sites that are really self-promotion sites for a product or service. While virtually all sites are selling something directly or promoting advertisers' products, some are more blatant than others. Some sites claim to offer free services, but when you go to those sites, you find only a catalog of products or services and nothing free at all.

Here is a list of <u>online financial news</u> sources:

<4financialnews.4anything.com>
<investorguide.com>
<news.ft.com>
<www.bloomberg.com>
<www.cyberinvest.com>
<www.investorama.com>
<www.moneynet.com>
<www.schwab.com>
<www.stockmaster.com>
<www.wallstreetcity.com>

The Bloomberg, Moneynet, and StockMaster sites are exceptionally well designed and provide a range of valuable news and information.

You can find information about individual companies, including free annual reports and links to corporate home pages at these Web sites:

<reportgallery.com>
<www.annualreportservice.com>
<www.prars.com>

Annual reports and corporation home pages are valuable sources for in-depth financial information. The quality and detail of the information varies by corporation, of course. However, if you are researching a company because you are thinking of buying its stock, its home page is a good starting point. If you already own a company's stock, its home page will help you find its quarterly and annual filings with the Securities and Exchange Commission (SEC). When you use a Web site, you get the information immediately, whereas waiting for the same information from an investor services department may take weeks.

PUTTING THE FINANCIAL NEWS TO WORK

Opinions are worthless, but facts are priceless. This market maxim summarizes well the realities of the financial media. Some financial organizations would like to believe that investors want to be told what to think. There is a particular arrogance associated with all news sources, financial and otherwise, that crosses the line between supplying information and telling the reader what to do with it. Many readers do want to be told what to think. However, in order to succeed as an investor, you must think for yourself. This could mean taking a contrarian approach, going against what everyone else thinks at the time.

> **KEY POINT:** One problem with placing too much trust
> in the financial news is that it is presents the most pop-
> ular version of how to think and what to do. Contrari-
> ans, however, are dubious about the validity of popular
> opinion; they would rather be right.

So we are left with two forces at work and interacting with
one another. On the one hand are financial reporters and journalists, and on the other hand are the readers. The journalists
are pressured to report stories in a particular manner, because
information must be conveyed quickly and efficiently; this
leaves little room for the in-depth analysis that more properly
belongs on the editorial page or in the research departments
of brokerage houses. Readers are in a quandary about how to
get reliable, timely information, but many readers want the
financial media to tell them what to think. They may not want
to take raw data and interpret it, they would rather be handed
the conclusion. No one can say what percentage of readers
feel this way; however, it is fair to speculate that the financial
media perceive this attitude to be widespread. Therefore the
media take upon themselves the task of identifying news as
positive or negative. They make their judgments on the basis
of some long-standing myths, such as:

- Growth is good, but nongrowth spells failure.
- Profit margins should expand from one year to the next
  without fail.
- People want to be told what to think and how to interpret
  the news
- The greater the growth in annual sales, the better.
- Readers are interested primarily in the averages and in
  identifying winners and losers.

These beliefs drive the financial media and dictate what gets
reported and what is left out of reports. Ironically, the financial news emphasizes short-term changes even though both

major market theories, the Dow Theory and the Random Walk Hypothesis, agree that short-term change is insignificant and unreliable, and state that short-term changes in price and volume cannot be used for analysis.

Daily and weekly papers report so frequently that it becomes necessary to emphasize short-term changes. A daily run-down of intermediate or long-term change would be repetitive and uninteresting from a journalistic point of view. Even though investors tend to be analytical by nature, we cannot expect every investor to study daily updates of intermediate trends with great anticipation and excitement. So the emphasis on the short term is not completely the reporter's fault. The emphasis is the result of pressure from the publication's management and advertising sales departments, adherence to sound reporting principles, and the demands of the reading public. As irrational as it is, investors who read the daily and weekly papers want to know what is happening in the DJIA, and they want the papers to tell them *why* it is happening. Even investors who identify themselves as believers in the fundamentals end up watching the averages and playing the game of prediction.

> **KEY POINT:** It is not enough to say that you believe in the fundamentals if, in fact, your emphasis is on trying to guess where the Dow Jones Industrial Average will be next year.

One of the best-known media sources for financial news is *Wall Street Week,* which is aired on PBS. The host and weekly guests engage in intelligent discussions about fundamentals and invariably claim that fundamental analysis is the key to identifying sound long-term investments. But the program often concludes with guests playing a guessing game about where the DJIA will be the following week or year. So even this very intellectual television program falls into the populist habit of predicting movements in the market average. It even refers to the DJIA as "the market" in its reporting.

All sources of financial news may be thought of as input to a comprehensive and analytical program. You have a portfolio of stocks you want to monitor, and you may have a short list of other stocks you might want to buy in the future. So in practice, you will be tracking only a handful of stocks or investment sectors. Thus, the general financial news will be of interest only insofar as it describes an overall mood of the market, pointing to a direction or sentiment that might or might not affect your individual holdings. You need to determine the effect of market sentiment on a stock-by-stock basis. You should get annual and quarterly reports for your investments and read them in full. This enables you to formulate an opinion based not only on what the PR department wants you to think, but also on what the numbers show concerning the company's health. It provides you with better insight and the means for comparison about the company's financial health. Form your own opinions about the stocks you are following, and don't accept interpretations in news stories as the last word. The raw data in the financial news is only the first word, the starting point for your process of analysis.

CHAPTER 2

Finding Your Own
Hidden Nuggets

We're drowning in information and starving for knowledge.

—Rutherford D. Rogers (*New York Times,* February 25, 1985)

The irony of modern stock market research is that even though there is so much information out there, very little of it is useful to you. The riverbed is awash in fool's gold, so to speak. Many an inexperienced investor has started out reading financial newspapers from cover to cover or surfing from Web site to Web site, collecting data, subscribing to services that sound the most promising, and slowly drowning in information. This approach is self-defeating.

The problem is not finding information; there is plenty of that available. The problem is identifying *good* information in the sea of useless news—gold nuggets in a riverbed full of worthless tidbits, empty promises, and faulty analysis. The North American financial press is superior to any other in the world, but the scope of the financial information is a problem as well as a great advantage.

You can depend on what you read to be accurate, as far as it goes, but without considerable effort, you cannot know how much of that information is useful to you in managing your portfolio. How helpful is it to study a daily half-hour break-down of levels in the Dow Jones Industrial Average (DJIA), or the number of new high and new low price levels reached by stocks last week, or which stocks gained or lost the biggest percentage in market price? These statistics do nothing to tell you if or when to buy, sell, hold, or stay away from the market. They are summaries of the broad market, and the market's changes may not be representative of what happens in your own portfolio. Your portfolio's performance depends on the stocks and other investments you have selected, the risks you are willing to take, and the specific strategies you employ.

> **KEY POINT:** The financial news provides a lot of infor-mation, but the important decisions you have to make require going beyond what is reported in the press.

A large part of the information provided in the financial press is of no specific value to you. Some broad analysis is help-ful in calculating and estimating the mood of the market, but the mood is only a generalized factor. The traditional mood indicators should be questioned critically anyway because they are flawed. For example, the price-earnings ratio (PE) might use very old financial information in comparison with today's stock price, making it unreliable and inaccurate. Cur-rent dividend yield is based on today's price, and not on the price that *you* paid for a stock. Even a stock's closing price is only that, the price at a specific moment in time. The current price might be much different—stocks rarely open the next day at exactly the level at which they closed. Even the method of reporting changes in stock prices is unreliable, because the number of points has a different meaning depending on a stock's price. A two-point rise is twice as significant for a $20 stock as it is for a $40 stock (a 10 percent change versus a 5 percent change).

The flaws in the traditional methods of reporting the financial news point the way toward becoming more effective at finding your hidden nuggets. It is just as important to know where *not* to look for important information as to know where to look. You can eliminate a large segment of information by knowing what provides you little or nothing of value. Six examples of popular information and sources that can be discounted or ignored are:

1. Market indexes and averages
2. Current dividend yield*
3. Stock charts
4. Short-term price changes of stocks
5. Internet advertising banners
6. Online chat rooms

Ironically, these are some of the more popular sources for information, which tells you why so many investors lose money. They are using sources of information that are inaccurate or unreliable, or that do not relate in any way to their own portfolios. Some investors are information junkies who enjoy spending time in chat rooms or studying price charts, but information junkies who make money in the market are rare. As a general rule, you can profit in the market only by doing intelligent research, staying within well-defined risk tolerance rules you set for yourself, and picking securities that make sense.

---

*While dividend income is important to large numbers of shareholders, the reported current yield of a stock is misleading. It is based on the dividend as a percentage of the stock's current market price, not of the price an individual investor paid for the stock. A more astute method for tracking dividend income is to compare your current dividend to the amount *you* originally paid for stock.

WHERE TO LOOK FOR HIDDEN NUGGETS

Once you know where not to look, you have narrowed the field of possibilities, and it becomes easier to find good information. So where are the hidden nuggets? Here are some good sources:

Current fundamental information. Acquire a company's current financial information by going directly to the corporation's Web site and obtaining the latest quarterly or annual report filed with the Securities and Exchange Commission (SEC). Take the time to identify a few useful and informative fundamental tests and apply these in yearly and quarterly comparative form. Among the typical fundamental tests you should include are trend analysis of sales and net profits; net earnings per share; and capitalization, notably any changes in debt capitalization from year to year. The latter is crucial, because as a corporation depends ever more heavily on debt, a growing portion of profits are then devoted to paying interest, which means less profit is available to continue or maintain dividend payments. Monitoring trends in dividend payment and yield is another important fundamental test to observe over many years. With all of this in mind, remember the validity of all fundamental tests can be judged only when analyzed in comparison with past periods, so that applicable trends can be observed.

Other useful fundamental tests include the company's position relative to its competitors within the company's sector; range of diversity in products or services; and information about insider trades, including whether corporate insiders are buying or selling shares. If the company is buying up its own shares and retiring them as treasury stock, for example, this tells you that the company's management believes the current stock price is a bargain. Get information directly from the company by logging on to the Internet and acquiring free annual reports. Many of the Web sites that offer free annual reports also provide links to the companies' home pages.

> **KEY POINT:** The fundamentals define long-term invest-ment potential. Because people place so much empha-sis on current stock price, they often overlook the less exciting but more valuable information found in the company's financial reports.

Analysis of a stock's investment value by established ser-vices. Some of the best overall analysis of stocks is provided by two well-established firms, Value Line and Standard & Poor's. Both of these organizations provide nicely detailed and regularly updated descriptions of stocks, identifying those that are the safest and most timely. They include current fun-damental and technical information; a narrative describing the company and its products or services; news of current interest to investors regarding contingent liabilities, labor relations, relative competitive positions, and more; and a good historical summary of sales and profits, dividends, and stock price.

> **KEY POINT:** The two major subscription services pro-vide reliable, detailed information to help investors to narrow their search. These services are valuable for comparisons between companies and for long-term col-lection of important fundamental and technical infor-mation.

Free online news and information sources. Online news and information is free and easy to find. If you perform a basic search online, you will be able to find an unlimited number of sources that will provide you with the day's stock news and with ongoing, wide-ranging analysis of companies and sectors. Just avoid the advertising banners and recognize that the information is there for free because advertisers are hoping you will visit their own Web sites.

> **KEY POINT:** All the news you need is free online. If anything, the vast array of information is a problem, because you have so much to choose from.

Brokerage company research reports. The major brokerage companies hire analysts to produce in-depth reports on many of the more popular companies (as well as companies in which the brokerage firm has taken a position in the stock). While their reports are intended for their own customers, it is quite easy to obtain copies of most of these reports; usually they are available from the company and are easily accessible online. However, some brokerage houses will restrict access and offer the reports only to their paying customers.

> **KEY POINT:** Brokerage companies provide in-depth research reports on selected companies and new issues. You might not have full access unless you become a paying customer.

To review brokerage Web sites, see Figure 2.1.

When selecting one brokerage site over another, look for the following three useful features:

1. Combination of text with graphics that makes it easy to use the site and to locate essential information
2. Inclusion of the day's financial news plus the current status of the major markets
3. Multiple uses for the site: easy reference to stock quotes and charts, a personal portfolio management section, and links to helpful information and news sites

Avoid pages that are difficult to use, overloaded with excessive ad banners, or too slow. Some sites slow down when market activity is especially high, and that is to be expected. But other sites are chronically slow, making them less practical and

---

FIGURE 2.1   Brokerage Web Sites

The following is a sample of some of the major brokerage firms' home pages:

<www.csfbdirect.com>
<www.etrade.com>
<www.goldmansachs.com>
<www.investment-center.hrblock.com>
<www.painewebber.com>
<www.mldirect.com>
<www.msdw.com>
<www.prusec.com>
<www.quick-reilly.com>
<www.schwab.com>
<www.smithbarney.com>

---

more prone to crashes during periods of high-volume market activity. The Web site for E*Trade and Schwab are exceptionally practical because they are well designed and highly accessible.

THE RESEARCHER'S CRITICAL EYE

A successful investor knows how to review information with a critical eye. This requires a degree of cynicism and suspicion, and a mind that is open to the possibility that new and valuable nuggets might be found at any moment. It is healthy to be suspicious of unsolicited offers, especially those that promise easy and fast riches—because that simply does not happen. However, it is possible to find good sources for information that you might have overlooked.

This is especially true online, where many free services and sources for information can help you save a lot of time and effort in your search for hidden nuggets. As a critical researcher, you should place a high value on your time and not waste it just looking for useful information. Whether you read books, study annual reports of listed companies, or surf the Web, you need to be able to dismiss useless information with great efficiency.

Use the following list of seven questions to determine whether a source of information is going to provide anything of value to you:

1. Is the information offered for free? If not, move on, unless it is information you believe you need, such as in-depth stock analysis.
2. Does the information concern stocks I am holding or am interested in for the future?
3. Does the source lead me to useful secondary sources of information (such as research papers or reports, stock charts, yield calculators, definitions, or resource links)?
4. Is the information sensible and realistic? If it includes promises of exciting new wealth opportunities, fast riches, or Wall Street secrets, pass it up.
5. Will a subscription entitle me to updated information? (Remember, in the market information gets old—and useless—very quickly.)
6. Does the source provide financial analysis I can use? (Many free quotation and charting services are valuable in this respect.)
7. Is the information broad or limited in scope? (Sources that provide only focused information are of limited use.)

As a critical researcher, you should be aware of the concepts long recognized by the major schools of thought on market analysis. These are the Dow Theory and the Random Walk Hypothesis (or Random Walk Theory). The Dow Theory recognizes three types of stock price movements: primary (major, or long-term), secondary, and daily. The Dow Theory also recognizes the following rules for predicting changes in the market: first, the Dow Jones Industrial Average and Dow Jones Transportation Average are used as predictors of primary movement; and second, to establish a reversal in the primary trend, a predictive movement in one average is confirmed by similar changes in the other.

The Random Walk Hypothesis, also known as the Efficient Market Hypothesis, states that a stock's current price reflects all information available about the stock at that moment. In other words, all stocks are priced fairly based on what investors know on that day. Thus, in any future movement the stock has a 50-50 chance of rising or falling.

Both of these schools of thought agree that short-term price change is useless as an indicator. Paying too much attention to the immediate news of the market, especially as it concerns changes in prices, is a misguided approach to research.

It makes more sense to select your investments on the basis of the fundamentals. You should pay attention to long-term growth potential and ignore short-term price changes. This can require nerves of steel, because many excellent long-term growth stocks experience short-term gyrations in price. Remember that as long as you have applied sound principles in the selection of a company, short-term pricing does not affect long-term value. Don't make the all-too-common mistake of reacting to today's news for the wrong reasons. Investors commonly make rash decisions, selling stock when the price falls, out of panic, and selling stock when the price rises, out of greed. These two forces—panic and greed—account for many of the lost opportunities in the market.

> **KEY POINT:** The advice to buy low and sell high may sound simplistic, but it is quite sensible once you realize that most investors do the opposite.

BECOMING A SHREWD ANALYST

As a market news reader, you must devote a good portion of your analytical skill to resisting the news itself. By its nature, the market news tends to tell the reader not only what is happening, but also what to think about it. It provides much useless information, including short-term price statistics, index and average movements, and stories with questionable angles. So as a shrewd analyst, you need to question all forms of news, and especially what you read on the financial pages.

> **KEY POINT:** Most people read the news and accept it passively. By researching beyond what you read in the news, you will improve the quality and value of your information.

As a successful investor, you will find the hidden nuggets by taking upon yourself the role of independent analyst. Avoid passively reading and accepting the financial news like most readers do. The vast majority of investors accept the premise that the DJIA is "the market," that they can stay informed by keeping up with current trends, including short-term price changes and each week's biggest winners and losers. But following unhelpful information and news is counterproductive and distracting. It takes up time that you could and should be spending looking for the useful information that you need to make intelligent decisions.

As a shrewd analyst, you know that the key to investing success is in finding information, interpreting it, and gaining insights that the typical investor does not have. All other subscribers have the same newspapers, so accepting what the financial press says means you have only the same information everyone else has. But in the market, the majority is wrong more often than it is right. The contrarian resists the herd mentality of the market because the market does not act upon intelligent information; it tends to overreact to rumor, gossip, and opinion. This makes the market as a whole a very unreliable source of information. Following the thoughts of the majority is a mistake.

The majority of investors react to short-term change, even when they call themselves long-term investors. They follow technical and speculative trends, and they pay attention to the

DJIA, stock charts, and high-low statistics, even though many of them define themselves as fundamentalists. The majority of investors look for insights about the market and spend a lot of time studying, then make their investment decisions on an irrational basis—movements in the DJIA, warnings from friends and coworkers, short-term price movements, or information from a single news story. Only the shrewd analyst will see the truth—that profit is the result of diligence and hard work. There are no shortcuts. If everyone could easily find the hidden nuggets, they would be worthless. The real value of above-average information is in its rarity. Following the crowd is no way to become rich.

DAY TRADING AND OTHER TECHNIQUES

Even the most shrewd analyst has to exercise self-discipline to avoid responding to popular trends. One of the most popular modern movements is day trading. This idea has captured the imagination of many investors, leading them into high-risk and speculative activity that can create sudden wealth *and* sudden, large losses.

Day trading is just that—high-volume trading in and out of stocks and other securities in very short-term increments of time, hours or even minutes. Day traders depend on momentary changes in prices to create profits. Because trading involves some cost, day traders have to trade in large blocks, often using derivatives to maximize profits. By using large block trading increments, the average fee per share charged by the brokerage firm is less. For example, if a firm charges a set minimum amount for a trade, the cost for 10,000 shares is substantially lower per share than a trade for 100 shares. Of course, block trades require placing much more capital at risk, which means a corresponding opportunity for profit *and* risk of loss. It is possible to make a lot of money in a very short period of time, but it is equally possible to lose it all, including the capital you cannot afford to lose.

Day trading is popular today because of the Internet. Traders have instant access to price-change information that was once available only to the true market insiders, brokers and floor traders. Now everyone can have online access to information and can become a player in the market. But day trading is a high-risk venture best left to professional speculators.

In the early 1980s the market was experiencing a continual upward movement in prices, and many investors had never lost any money in the market. When the large price drop took place in October 1986, investors were taken by surprise. Those who had entered the market at its peak lost large amounts of money, and speculators who had leveraged their capital by using brokers' margin accounts lost more than they could afford. The same outcome is not only likely, but inevitable, given the frenzy of day trading activity. It's just a matter of time. As more and more speculators become day traders, greed becomes the driving force and players take ever-growing chances, forgetting that losses can happen just as quickly as gains. They eventually learn the gambler's hard lessons:

1. Hindsight is always better than foresight.
2. It would have been better to fold one trade sooner.
3. You have to know not only how much you can profit, but also what you are risking.

Day trading is just a get-rich-quick scheme, the latest in a long line of market frenzies dating back to the days of tulip-mania.* When markets are hot, most people do not recognize the danger; whether they're trading stocks, gold, or tulips, greed takes over. Ultimately, the failure to recognize risk leads to large losses that always take the speculator by surprise.

---

*In seventeenth-century Holland, tulips became so valuable that speculators paid huge fortunes for a single bulb of a particular rarity. They were traded actively on the major stock exchanges until the whole market collapsed and thousands of investors lost everything.

It seems that there is never a shortage of gimmicks or tricks in the market. Once you get your name on the mailing lists, you will receive dozens of unsolicited offers from a broad range of companies, whether online or via snail mail. Some will be subscription offers from well-established financial newspapers or analytical services, but many more will be from companies offering some form of money-making scheme—unpublished secrets of wealth, a new formula to double your capital in one week or less, and other such promises. None of the junk-mail offers will deliver what they promise. No one has gotten rich by paying for a subscription to a newsletter that promises to show its readers how to get rich. Market success is not something you can buy for $39.95, it is something that you earn with your own thoughtful study, hard work, and good planning.

Avoid the allure of the "easy way" to get rich on Wall Street. It doesn't exist. People who have made a fortune in the market have taken chances in order to succeed, to be sure; but they have also recognized real value and have made decisions at the right time after intelligent analysis and study. It might be possible to get rich overnight with an impulsive and ill-studied decision, but if you are wrong, you won't have the capital to try again. Are you willing to take that chance?

Wise investors must separate the hidden nuggets from the fool's gold of misleading concepts. (See Figure 2.2.) Outright securities fraud is at least as common online as it was before the days of the Internet. You must exercise caution and protect your financial records. This means following sound principles: Never give out your password, Social Security number, or other investment information to anyone who contacts you. Be aware that the whole business of investing involves money, so it attracts the con artist as much as it attracts the idealist who wants to realize the American dream. With so many false leads and promises online, everyone has to be careful. The regulatory agencies do a fine job, but they cannot keep up with the ever-evolving frauds that con artists develop in order to take money from unsuspecting investors.

FIGURE 2.2   Checklist for Finding Hidden Nuggets

---

1. Read the financial news with cynicism.

2. Research further on your own, and never take a financial news story as the last word.

3. Use financial information as raw data for further research.

4. Confirm all news independently with a second source.

5. Get free information online. Download and read annual reports and the quarterly reports that listed companies file with the SEC.

6. Become an expert at reading and interpreting financial statements.

7. Remember that analysts might impose unrealistic expectations on the outcomes outlined in financial reports. Companies need not expand sales to succeed, and it is unrealistic to expect ever-increasing net yields. Reckless expansion can cause a disaster.

8. Do not pay for subscriptions to publications that promise to show you how to get rich.

9. Recognize the limitations of financial listings. Items like price-earnings ratio (PE) and dividend yield do not help you to track your portfolio; you need current information.

10. Remember that although the financial news usually reports changes in stock price as the number of points of the change, the significant number is the *percent* increase or decrease.

11. View broad indexes and averages as interesting statistical information, but don't make investment decisions based on them. Your portfolio is not going to follow movements in the indexes.

12. If you monitor stock charts, avoid the trap of believing that price patterns can predict near-term price movement. Some charting concepts are useful, but you need more than charts to make informed investment decisions.

13. Stay away from highly speculative techniques like day trading. Every high-opportunity investment brings high-risk exposure.

14. Finally, remember that your investment decisions are yours alone. Avoid investing on the basis of what the majority thinks or does.

The modern investor cannot blame poor investment results on the lack of information. With newspapers, subscription services, magazines, and brokerage firm analyses available, and a vast library of free information on the Internet, there is plenty of opportunity for research. The investor's biggest problem is in identifying the hidden nuggets within the larger array of data. You can lose money by simply using the wrong information to make your investment decisions. You succeed by doing smart analysis and comprehensive risk evaluation. You avoid mistakes by recognizing not only the value of financial news, but also its limitations. Any time you are using a source everyone else is using, the real value of your source is limited. You will find the hidden nuggets by going beyond the raw data. It is not enough to get the basic information. To gain real profits you must take the next step.

CYNIC — One who attributes all actions to selfish motives.

CHAPTER 3

Stock Market Listings

Never invest your money in anything that eats
or needs repainting.

  –Billy Rose (*New York Post*, October 26, 1957)

Information is the key to your success. Every investor requires up-to-date, dependable information that reveals the
ever-changing status of listed stocks, bonds, mutual funds, and
other publicly traded investments.

But there is so much information. Daily listings of all of the
security products available on all of the public exchanges are
comprehensive and highly detailed, and only a very small portion of the information is of interest to any one individual
investor. Your task is to find your way through the news and
listings and to identify only a few salient items:

- Updated listings for your current holdings
- Updated listings for stocks and other investments you are
  thinking of buying
- Relevant news and information about specific companies
  that interest you
- Broader market news affecting the sector or companies
  you follow

In addition, you need to be able to determine what the financial-page listings actually mean—you need to know how to translate the raw data into meaningful and revealing facts that may affect your decision to buy, sell, or hold a particular investment. This is not a simple task, considering the scope and complexity of the financial news.

> **KEY POINT:** Raw data, by itself, is not particularly useful, but it reveals information that you can use to develop market insights.

With the widespread availability of online information, it now is possible to acquire daily updated listings for individual stocks free of charge. You can review daily charts of price and volume changes, obtain current information about important fundamental and technical indicators, and update your portfolio with only minor delays. In the past you would need to subscribe to a daily paper or depend on telephone calls to a brokerage firm. Today's global electronic market is far more efficient, and much of the information you need and want is available without charge. In the following pages, I present a detailed examination of stock listings, explaining what each item of information tells you—and of equal importance, what it does not tell you—and how the information can be misunderstood.

REPORTING STOCK PRICES: THE CHANGE TO DECIMALIZATION

As this book is being written, all of the major stock exchanges are undergoing a change from the traditional practice of reporting prices using fractions of a dollar, to reporting prices in a dollars-and-cents format. This change, intended to make the math of investing less confusing, is called decimalization, and the transition is a multi-year process scheduled to be completed in 2002 or 2003. A stock price that was once reported as 35⅜ will now be reported as 35.38 ($35.37½ rounded to the nearest cent).

FIGURE 3.1   Fractions and Decimal Equivalents

FRACTION	DECIMAL
¹⁄₁₆	0.06
¹⁄₈	0.13
³⁄₁₆	0.19
¹⁄₄	0.25
⁵⁄₁₆	0.31
³⁄₈	0.38
⁷⁄₁₆	0.44
¹⁄₂	0.50
⁹⁄₁₆	0.56
⁵⁄₈	0.63
¹¹⁄₁₆	0.69
³⁄₄	0.75
¹³⁄₁₆	0.81
⁷⁄₈	0.88
¹⁵⁄₁₆	0.94

The practice of trading in eighths can be traced to colonial times, when the Spanish monetary system was the prevalent exchange medium. The "pieces of eight" of Spanish money became the standard, and American money continues to be influenced by the Spanish system. A quarter often is called "two bits," which is ²⁄₈ of a dollar, or two pieces of eight. Change takes time; today, centuries later, the American stock exchanges are slowly updating to the more easily understood decimal system.

> **KEY POINT:** Fractional values can be confusing and even misleading. Decimalization uses dollars and cents to help clarify valuation.

Figure 3.1 summarizes common market fractions and their decimal equivalent values.

To convert a fraction to a decimal, simply divide the numerator (top part of the fraction) by the denominator (bottom part

---

FIGURE 3.2   Converting a Fraction to Its Decimal Equivalent

$$\frac{\text{Numerator}}{\text{Denominator}} = \text{Decimal equivalent}$$

$$\frac{5}{8} = 0.63$$

---

of the fraction). The answer is the decimal equivalent. The formula is summarized in Figure 3.2.

Decimalization will cause some confusion. Investors will need to adjust their ways of thinking, so they may resist at first; however, because the money system is in decimal form, it makes sense to report dollar values of stock in dollars and cents, rather than in fractions.

KEY POINT: Decimalization will improve understanding of pricing. The older fractional method is inefficient and misleading.

MARKET LISTINGS—NYSE AND NASDAQ

The New York Stock Exchange (NYSE) has been in existence since 1792, and today it has the highest capitalization of any exchange. Many of the biggest and oldest corporations in the United States are listed on the NYSE. The best-known market index, the Dow Jones Industrial Average (DJIA), emphasizes change in price for stocks listed on the NYSE, which is widely considered to be "the market" even though more stock listings are found on the Nasdaq.

KEY POINT: A detailed history of the NYSE, as well as current information and statistics, can be found at the NYSE home page *<www.nyse.com>*.

The Nasdaq (the National Association of Securities Dealers Automated Quotations) was formed in 1971 as the first electronic stock exchange. It specializes in over-the-counter (OTC) stocks, stocks that are not listed on other, physical exchanges.

In 1998, the Nasdaq and the American Stock Exchange merged, forming the Nasdaq-AMEX Group. The group lists over 5,000 OTC stocks, the companies that were previously listed on Amex, and more than 400 foreign companies. Nasdaq and AMEX stocks are still reported separately in stock listings.

KEY POINT: For more information about the Nasdaq and its members, check their Web site at *<nasdaq.com>*.

The typical stock listing provides a wealth of information. We will use the listings provided in the biggest daily financial newspaper, the *Wall Street Journal,* as our starting point; then we will compare the *Journal* to other publications and listing formats.

The *Journal's* NYSE, Nasdaq, and AMEX listings show 12 specific pieces of information on each line:

1. 52-week high price
2. 52-week low price
3. Stock name
4. Trading symbol
5. Dividend
6. Yield
7. PE ratio
8. Volume
9. High price for the day
10. Low price for the day
11. Closing price
12. Price change

A daily listing for Eastman Kodak is shown in Figure 3.3. Note that the listing appears in both decimal and fractional form, so you can review both formats.

FIGURE 3.3 New York Stock Exchange Listing

The Wall Street Journal

(Fractional)

78⁹⁄₃₂	53³⁄₁₆	EKodak	EK	1.76	3.0	12	16158	58¾	56¹³⁄₁₆	58⅛	+1³⁄₁₆

(Decimal)

78.28	53.19	EKodak	EK	1.76	3.0	12	16158	58.75	56.81	58.13	+1.19

Each of these bits of information reveals a lot about the stock's history and current price status:

1. and 2. *52-week high and low prices.* During the past one-year period, Eastman Kodak's price ranged between $53.19 and $78.28 per share. This information not only shows the historical trading range, but also the volatility of the stock. A high-volatility stock is considered more risky than a low-volatility stock. To compute volatility, first find the difference between the 52-week high and the 52-week low price, then divide the result by the 52-week low. The answer is expressed as a percentage. This is summarized in Figure 3.4.

   The 52-week price range also reveals where the stock's current price stands in relation to its overall trading range for the year. In this example, the current price of $58.13 per share is near the low end of the trading range.

3. *Stock name.* Each stock is identified uniquely by its company name so two different company's listings will not be confused. Eastman Kodak's summary, EKodak, distinguishes it from companies, like EK Cher Motorcycle, that have similar names and trading symbols.

4. *Trading symbol.* Every listed stock is further identified with a unique symbol that has two to three characters. Eastman Kodak is identified as EK. This distinctive symbol is important not only because you can use it to distinguish one printed listing from another, but also because

---

FIGURE 3.4   Volatility

$$\frac{\text{High price} - \text{Low price}}{\text{Low price}} = \text{Volatility}$$

$$\frac{78.28 - 53.19}{53.19} = 47.2\%$$

---

you can use it to obtain free quotes online. The unique symbol distinguishes Eastman Kodak from all other listed stocks, including EK Chor Motorcycle, whose trading symbol is EKC.

5. *Dividend.* The dividend figure is the dollar value of dividends paid per share. In the case of Eastman Kodak, each shareholder received $1.76 per share. The reported amount is normally based on the most recently declared dividend. Payments of dividends usually occur quarterly; you can divide the reported amount by four to arrive at each quarterly distribution. In Eastman Kodak's case, the $1.76 annual dividend would be paid out as 44 cents per share each quarter.

6. *Yield.* The yield is the percentage of return to investors for the dividends declared. It is calculated by dividing the dividend (previous column) by the latest price per share (second-to-last column). In the current example, the dividend of $1.76 per share is divided by the current price per share, $58.13:

$$1.76 \div 58.13 = 3.0\%$$

7. *PE ratio.* The PE ratio is a popular and widely used indicator that provides a comparative evaluation of the stock's current price in relation to the earnings of the company. To find PE, divide the current price by earnings per share (EPS). The EPS for a company is found weekly in the stock listings published by *Barron's*. The

number can also be found on any number of sites online. For example, Quote.com lists current information for a stock, including pricing per share (both numerically and on a chart), volume, PE, and EPS, among other indicators. PE reflects the current perception of future value, or growth potential. As a general rule, higher-than-average PE reflects greater risk *and* greater potential for growth; lower PE indicates greater safety and price stability.

8. *Volume.* Each day's trading volume also provides good comparative data for evaluating a stock's popularity in the market. Of course, because the majority of trades in companies like Eastman Kodak are executed by mutual funds, the study of the volume figure by itself could be misleading. Volume is reported in hundreds, meaning that the last two digits of the volume amount are left off. In the case of Eastman Kodak, 16158 translates to 1,615,800 shares traded during the reported day. When the volume is accompanied by the letter *f,* it tells you that the last four digits have been excluded.

9. *High price for the day.* This dollar value per share represents the highest price at which the stock traded during the reported day. Along with the following column, it provides you with the day's trading range.

10. *Low price for the day.* This dollar value is the lowest price at which the stock traded that day. In the case of EK, the trading range for the day was between a high of $58.75 per share and a low of $56.81 per share, a range of just under $2.00.

11. *Closing price.* This is the value most people find the most interesting, the price at which the stock closed at the end of the day's trading. EK closed at $58.13 per share.

12. *Price change.* This shows the size and direction of change, with + for upward movement and – for downward movement. EK closed up $1.19 per share for the reported day.

FIGURE 3.5 Earnings and Dividend Reports, NYSE Stocks

				Barron's			
12/99	4.33	5.64	6.23	Jun1.65	1.52	q.44	09-01-00

The *Wall Street Journal* also includes several symbols to further advise you about the status of each of the stocks listed. The additional symbols are explained in a table usually located on the page preceding the NYSE listings.

> **KEY POINT:** Much of the *Wall Street Journal*'s financial news and information can be accessed online at *<www.wsj.com>*.

Sometimes a listing in the *Wall Street Journal* is boldfaced or underlined. A boldfaced listing indicates that the current price has changed by 5 percent or more (if the previous price was $2 per share or higher). An underlined listing indicates that the trading volume has changed significantly. More explanation of these highlighted listings are provided in the explanatory notes section that precedes the daily listings.

The *Wall Street Journal* is published by the Dow Jones Company. Another paper from the same publisher, *Barron's,* is published once a week, and it provides a weekly summary of the information found in the *Wall Street Journal. Barron's* summarizes price changes and reports earnings and dividend information for each listed stock. The content of the *Barron's* listings appears in Figure 3.5. *Barron's* provides the same format for information in its AMEX listings.

These columns show the following about Eastman Kodak:

1. *Latest year reported.* In the example, earnings are being reported for the full year ending December 1999.
2. *Year's earnings per share.* This shows the earnings for the full year on a per-share basis. In the case of EK, stockholders earned $4.33 per share of stock last year.

3. *Current year's estimate of earnings per share.* This column reports estimated earnings per share for the current year. EK's estimate for 2000 was $5.64 per share.

4. *Next year's estimate of earnings per share.* This column reports estimated earnings per share for the following year. EK projected earnings in 2001 of $6.23 per share.

5. *Most recent quarterly earnings per share.* In the quarter ending in June 2000, EK's shareholders earned $1.65 per share.

6. *Quarterly earnings one year ago.* This column shows the quarterly earnings for the same quarter in the previous year. EK's earnings were $1.52 per share in 1999's second quarter.

7. *Latest dividend.* The second-to-last column shows the dividend per share and frequency of payment. EK has most recently declared a quarterly dividend of $.44 per share.

8. *Record date.* This shows the dividend record date. Shareholders were paid a dividend on the number of shares they owned as of that date; if shares were sold before that date, the new owners were entitled to the dividend. In EK's case, all shareholders were entitled to dividend payments on shares they owned as of September 1, 2000.

KEY POINT: Much of *Barron's* financial news and information can be accessed online at *<www.barrons.com>*. *Barron's* also offers free access to annual reports (and current quarterly reports, if available) for listed companies. When ordering, have the stock's trading symbol ready. This service is available by telephone (U.S. callers 800-965-2929; international callers 804-272-1968) or by fax (800-747-9384). Annual reports can be ordered online at *<www.worldinvestorlink.com>*.

Barron's includes a full page each week entitled "How to Read the *Barron's* Stock Tables." This summarizes the use of

FIGURE 3.6 New York Stock Exchange Listing

Investor's Business Daily

(Fractional)													
89	59	E	A	C	70¼	Wal-Mart	WMT	54⁹⁄₁₆	–3/8	+59	9.0m	42	54¹⁵⁄₁₆	53

(Decimal)													
89	59	E	A	C	70.25	Wal-Mart	WMT	54.56	–0.38	+59	9.0m	42	54.94	53

symbols and codes. *Barron's* does not use underlining or bold-face highlighting like the *Wall Street Journal;* it substitutes specific symbols to indicate the important changes in a stock's price and volume.

Competing with the *Wall Street Journal* is another daily paper, *Investor's Business Daily (IBD)*. Listings for NYSE issues are quite different in this publication. *Investor's Business Daily* provides many more fundamental and technical ratings and uses highlighting to make the listings easy to absorb. A typical *Investor's Business Daily* NYSE listing is shown in Figure 3.6. (Listings for American Stock Exchange stocks are shown in the same format.)

These columns report the following 15 forms of information about each listed stock:

1. *Earnings per share rating.* This rating compares each stock to the market as a whole in terms of EPS. In the example, Wal-Mart's EPS rating was 89, meaning Wal-Mart's earnings outperformed the earnings of 89 percent of other listed companies.
2. *Relative price strength rating.* This indicator shows the calculated 12-month price performance compared to other stocks. It may be a negative value, for stocks whose price fell over the past year. In the example, Wal-Mart was rated at 59, meaning its price in the past year outperformed the price of 59 percent of other stocks.
3. *Industry group relative strength rating.* Nearly 200 industry groups are evaluated according to five catego-

ries of performance over a six-month period. An *A* indicates that the stock's industry performed in the top 20 percent, and an *E* means the industry performed in the bottom 20 percent. Wal-Mart's rating was *E,* meaning that Wal-Mart's industry group was among the lowest-rated for the previous six months.

4. *Sales plus profit margin plus return on investment rating.* Companies are compared according to their performance on four important fundamentals: sales growth rate, pretax profit, after-tax profit, and return on equity. Wal-Mart's rating was *A,* meaning its fundamentals placed it in the top 20 percent of stocks.

5. *Accumulation/distribution rating.* This summarizes the last 13 weeks of buying and selling levels in the stock, taking into account price and volume. Ratings of *A* and *B* indicate heavy to moderate buying. A rating of *C* is assigned when buying and selling are balanced. Ratings of *D* and *E* are used for stocks experiencing moderate to heavy selling. Wal-mart's status was neutral: it had a *C* rating.

6. *52-week high.* The *Investor's Business Daily* listings show the 52-week high, but not the low. When "nh" appears in this column, it means a new high occurred on that day. If the stock's closing price is within 10 percent of the 52-week high, then the 52-week high is boldfaced. Wal-Mart's 52-week high was $70.25 per share.

7. and 8. *Stock name and stock symbol.* These two columns have the same information as other publication's listings. Wal-Mart's trading symbol is WMT.

9. and 10. *Closing price and price change.* These two items are reported in the same manner as they are in other sources.

11. *Volume percentage change.* This is the percentage above or below each stock's average trading volume for the past 50 trading days. This column enables you to spot stocks whose volume has changed significantly. If the change is 50 percent or more, this item is boldfaced.

Wal-Mart's volume was boldfaced on the day in question because its trading volume was 59 percent higher than its 50-day average.

12. *Volume.* As in other sources, volume is reported in hundreds of shares. If the volume is followed by an *m*, it means millions rather than hundreds of shares. Wal-Mart's volume was 9.0m, meaning 9 million shares were traded.

13. *PE ratio.* As in other sources, this popular rating is derived by dividing the current price per share by the latest-reported earnings per share. Wal-Mart's PE on the day reported was 42.

14. and 15. *Day's high price and day's low price.* Unlike the *Wall Street Journal, Investor's Business Daily* places these figures that provide the day's trading range at the end of the listing. The difference between Wal-Mart's high and low for the day was $1.94 per share.

Special highlighting helps you to identify important changes in listings. Boldfaced issues are those whose price is at a new high or is up one point or more on the day. Those stocks that have a new low price or are down one point or more are underlined. Stocks that are boldfaced *and* italicized are newer issues (less than eight years old) that have EPS ratings and relative price strength ratings of 80 or higher. With these highlighting tools, it is easy to scan the *Investor's Business Daily* listings and quickly spot the major performers of the day. Unlike other financial papers, *Investor's Business Daily* also offers abbreviated listings—including only stock name and symbol; dividend; yield; volume; last price; and net change.

KEY POINT: More information is available about *Investor's Business Daily* at the paper's Web site, *<www .investors.com>.*

IBD includes an additional valuable feature at the beginning of its NYSE and Nasdaq listings: its highlighted "Stocks in the News." This is usually a half-page compilation of charts for stocks that have reached price and volume milestones—issues trading over $12 per share that have hit new price high levels and issues trading over $15 that have risen a half-point or more per share and have had the greatest percentage increase in volume.

The same information is shown for AMEX listings, although in general, fewer of those stocks are highlighted. Included are stocks trading over $5 per share that have hit new price highs or are trading near a new high, and those issues trading over $15 that have the greatest increase in volume and at least a half-point increase in price. The nine-month charts show volume, a weekly breakdown of price with moving average, and a very brief description of the company.

Instructions on how to read these sections appears in *IBD* every other Friday.

INTERNATIONAL STOCK REPORTS

For international investing, the *London Times* offers a business section that lists the top 200 British-listed companies and summarizes world markets by index. The major indicator used in the *London Times* is the Financial Times Stock Exchange (FTSE, pronounced "footsie"), which was developed jointly by the *Financial Times* and the London Stock Exchange, Limited.

Another international financial news source is the *Financial Times,* which is based in London and is also published in New York and other major world cities. It includes nicely detailed world stock market listings that include important stocks sold in the major exchanges in North America, South America, Europe, Asia, Africa, and Australia. The paper summarizes London Stock Exchange dealings; lists options, currency rates, commodities, and managed fund (mutual fund) companies; and it includes a highly detailed listing of all European markets.

The London Stock Exchange's Web site provides additional information about its organization and the more than 2,750 stocks it trades (including 500 stocks in the United Kingdom). Its address is *<www.londonstockexchange.com>*.

> ◤ **KEY POINT:** International Web sites of interest:
>
> More information about the *London Times* can be found on its Web site at *<www.the-times.co.uk>*.
>
> The London Stock Exchange's Web site provides additional information about its organization and the more than 2,750 stocks it trades (including 500 stocks in the United Kingdom). Its address is *<www.london stockexchange.com>*.
>
> For additional information about the FTSE, check *<www.ft-se.co.uk>*.
>
> For more information about the *Financial Times* and its services, check its Web site at *<news.ft.com>*.

The *Wall Street Journal* summarizes details for selected stocks on all major world exchanges in a half-page "Foreign Markets" table. In the same section is a listing of stock market indexes from around the world and an overview of world stock markets that includes news briefs, Dow Jones global indexes, and an industry-specific listing of leading and lagging global groups. Closing prices of stocks within the global groups are reported, as well as the change in price and the percentage of that change. Stock prices are listed in U.S. currency values. *Barron's* also provides a weekly summary of the Dow Jones global indexes and editorial and news discussions of overseas stocks. Special sections concentrate on European and Asian market news. A nicely detailed weekly summary of foreign markets, listed by country, also appears, along with a summary of the week's action in global stock markets and indexes.

FIGURE 3.7   Daily Status Table

USA Today
Most Widely Held Stocks

			Pctg. Change	
Stock	**Thurs.**	**Chg.**	**Day**	**Year**
AT&T	23.75	−1.50	−5.9	−53.3
America Online	51.00	−3.50	−6.4	−32.8
Cisco Systems	49.81	−1.38	−2.7	− 7.1
ExxonMobil	94.13	+0.38	+0.4	+16.8

OTHER SOURCES FOR FINANCIAL NEWS

Most daily papers include a breakdown of the stock listings, but some appear in abbreviated fashion and most are for the NYSE listings only. Very few daily papers have space to devote to comprehensive listings such as those in the specialized financial press.

Most daily papers are also local by nature; even the largest daily papers in major cities in the United States and Canada tend to use wire services to cover international news and are otherwise highly local. Their financial news sections tend to emphasize stocks of regional interest.

One national daily paper, *USA Today,* provides national coverage of the financial markets in its "Money" section, which usually runs 12 pages. The section includes current news about the stock market and is more comprehensive than the financial sections of most regional and local newspapers. *USA Today* provides a full page summarizing market news and presenting tables showing the status of stock indexes, the most widely held stocks, the stocks that are most active after hours, and foreign markets. A typical partial daily listing in the *USA Today* status tables is shown in Figure 3.7.

This information includes:

1. *Stock name.* The stock name identifies the company.

FIGURE 3.8 NYSE Listing

USA Today

52-Week		Stock	Div	PE	Last	Change
High	**Low**	**Stock**	**Div**	**PE**	**Last**	**Change**
67.00	26.21	NewsCorp	.07e	37	43.56	−1.94

2. *Ending price for the most recent day.* This is the closing price per share of stock. *USA Today* is far ahead of most other papers in reporting stock price information in decimal form.

3. *Change.* This column shows the price change since the previous day in decimal form.

4. and 5. *Percentage change columns.* These columns show the percentage of change in stock price for the reported day and year to date. This *percentage* change in the stock price, generally ignored by other financial news sources, is far more revealing than the point change, which has varying significance depending on the stock's price. (For example, a three-point drop for a $60 stock is a 5 percent change, whereas a three-point drop for a $15 stock is a 20 percent change.)

USA Today also reports briefly on international currency rates, consumer interest rates, and mutual funds, and it lists the NYSE stocks in summarized form, giving decimal values for all dollar amounts. A typical *USA Today* stock listing is shown in Figure 3.8.

These columns provide the following:

1. and 2. *52-week high and low price.* The first two columns show the high and low value of stock in the past 52 weeks.

3. *Stock name.* The name of the company is listed next. The company in our example is NewsCorp.

4. *Dividend.* This is the dividend per share. In the example, NewsCorp has declared a dividend of seven cents per share. The *e* following the dividend amount indicates that the dividend was declared or paid during the past 12 months. If this qualifier is absent, the dividend per share represents annual payout during the past year.
5. *PE ratio.* The latest available PE is shown next. News-Corp's PE is 37.
6. *Last price.* This is the closing price of the stock for the day reported. In the example, NewsCorp closed at $43.56 per share.
7. *Change.* The last column reports the change in price per share since the previous day. NewsCorp closed down $1.94 per share.

USA Today also provides Nasdaq and AMEX listings that show 52-week high and low, stock name, last price, and change from the previous day. For all stock listings, boldfaced print is used for stocks that rose or fell by 5 percent or more. The paper also includes a table of stock footnotes.

KEY POINT: To check listings online, go to the *USA Today* home page at *<markets.usatoday.com>*.

INTERPRETING THE LISTINGS

The information provided in the typical stock listing seems straightforward, but it requires interpretation. In many respects, the way that financial information is reported can distort what is happening to a stock. You need to know how to translate the information so that it can be used accurately.

Several of the items of raw data in a stock listing are often misleading.

52-week high and low prices. The high and low price of the stock give you a 52-week trading range that can mean several different things. Consider the differences among these three scenarios:

1. The stock began the year at its 52-week low, climbed to its high, and then fell back to near its low point.
2. The stock began at or near its high point, had a brief mid-year plunge, then immediately settled into a relatively narrow trading range, where it remained for the rest of the year.
3. The stock began the year near its low point, has been climbing steadily for the entire year, and is now trading near its 52-week high.

These three scenarios paint entirely different pictures of the stock's recent history. However, these variations will not show up in the raw data provided in each day's listing. Thus, the reported information is incomplete, and you cannot use it reliably without doing further research. A good starting point is to get the stock's 52-week price chart.

KEY POINT: To obtain a 52-week price chart, use one of the many free online charting services and select the full-year chart option. One company that provides this free service is Charles Schwab & Company at *<www.schwab.com>*. This site provides many charting options, and the charts include a moving average, which is helpful in determining an accurate historical trading range.

The 52-week high/low often is used to calculate volatility, the measurement of a stock's safety based on its historical trading range. But obviously, the many possible scenarios that create the trading range have to be considered as well. Volatility calculations will be more reliable if unusual price spikes are removed and if volatility is reviewed along with an analysis of price on the basis of moving average.

Moving average is a form of averaging that is used in trend analysis. A simple average involves adding up the values in a field and dividing by the number of values. For example, the simple average of 7, 9, 12, and 14 is 10.5. This is computed by adding up the four values and then dividing by 4:

$$\frac{7 + 9 + 12 + 14}{4} = 10.5$$

The use of average is widespread in all forms of financial analysis. Moving average irons out the peaks and valleys of a larger field of values (like stock prices), so that the long-term trend is more easily viewed. The removal of unusual spikes avoids distortions. For example, if a stock's price has ranged between 20 and 26 for the past year, that is a fairly narrow trading range and volatility would be low. A single dip to 14 may be excluded from the moving average in some cases. Also, a widespread market drop tends to affect all stocks, often with price change overreactions; thus removing the exceptional price changes would be appropriate.

Moving average can involve the use of a larger number of fields or only a few. For example, a stock price's moving average could be reported daily using a full year's closing stock prices. As a general rule, the more fields used, the more stable the moving average appears. Such calculations can be managed through automated systems but would be daunting to perform manually, even though the formula is not complex. Each period's new moving average involves dropping off the oldest value and adding on the newest. So for a moving average involving a full year of approximately 245 trading days, each day's average would be the average of 245 closing prices. The following day would be calculated by dropping off the oldest day's closing price, adding in the latest day's closing price, and then dividing the new total by the number of trading days in the year (245).

Yield. The reported dividend yield can create problems for investors if they are not aware of how to use the data. The yield changes every day because it is calculated on the basis of the current closing price. But the dividend to be paid per share usually is declared and fixed in advance, so as the stock's price falls, the yield rises. For example, if Eastman Kodak pays $1.76 per share for the coming year, the yield at different stock prices varies:

Price	Yield
$38	4.6%
48	3.7
58	3.0
68	2.6
78	2.3

Yield is higher when the stock's price is lower, and vice versa. This method of calculating dividend yield does not result in reliable information for tracking stock you already own. It only reveals the yield you would earn from dividends if you were to buy stock at the current closing price. Once you own a share of the stock, the daily report of dividend yield is useless to you. You should only calculate the yield you actually receive, using your basis (the price you paid for the stock plus trading fees) and the dividend being paid per share.

PE ratio. The price-earnings ratio is the source of much controversy. In some respects, it is an ideal indicator because it quantifies a stock's market value in terms of a fundamental characteristic, the earnings per share. The higher the PE, the higher the market's perception that the stock's price will grow and that the stock is fundamentally strong in terms of earnings per share. The PE is expressed as a multiple of earnings, so the higher the PE, the greater the market's expectations for future performance. Some market watchers believe higher-PE stocks outperform lower-PE stocks, but studies have revealed that the opposite is true. The market creates the high PE through buying demand. As the price is driven upward, the PE increases as well. If the price is too high, a correction can be expected at some point. Thus, a higher-PE stock, while highly interesting and popular in the market, also can be more volatile than the average stock.

Another problem with relying on PE too much is that the information might be out of date. Price, of course, is always current, and PE is calculated on the basis of the day's market price. However, the earnings per share information might be very out of date. The longer the time since the most recent financial report, the less reliable the PE ratio because the current price is being compared to very old information. This is a point often ignored by market analysts and investors. Because a lot of change might have taken place in the corporation's current quarter, old information should be highly discounted. This is especially true for corporations whose earnings have been inconsistent in the past. Before placing much value in the PE ratio, first find out how old the earnings per share is, and then use or discount the information accordingly.

Volume. The number of shares traded during a period can be quite revealing; however, it means different things depending on whether the stock is rising or falling. In the auction market, every transaction has a buyer and a seller, so high volume represents activity on both sides. You need to ask yourself: Is that volume driven by buying activity or by selling activity? The stock's price direction establishes the answer on days when there is significant point-value change; however, a stock can also experience high volume with little or no change in value. What does it mean when that happens?

In some situations, it can mean that an institutional investor, such as a mutual fund, is buying or selling shares of that particular stock on the day in question. Because institutional trading represents the majority of trading volume, it is fair to say that a study of institutional trading reveals much more than a study of the action among individuals, also called *retail inves-*

tors. If an institutional investor is transacting heavily in the stock of one company but the price is not changing very much as a result, that indicates that the stock has a lot of price strength at that level. This is useful information for you if you own the stock or are thinking of buying shares. However, just watching volume levels and changes—without further investigation—does not reveal much information at all.

Price change. To many investors, the most important question is that of how many points a stock changed, and in what direction. However, the traditional reporting by numbers of points is unreliable and misleading. Most people believe that a four-point change in a stock's price is significant, especially when compared to a mere one-point change in another stock on the same day. But is it necessarily significant?

Consider the case of a $90-per-share stock that moves up four points, compared to a $20 stock that moves up only one point. Which is returning more to the investor? If you invest $9,000 in 100 shares of the higher-priced stock, a four-point increase represents a 4.4 percent return. However, if you invest $2,000 in 100 shares of the lower-priced stock, a one-point move is a 5 percent return—a half-point better than the four-point move in the higher-priced stock. It is more accurate to report price changes as a percentage of the previous day's price. This is not done by most financial news sources, however, so the point-based reporting has to be taken with great caution. Be aware of what's happening to your investment in the stock, and pay less attention to point movement.

Your real percentage of return is going to be affected by your original basis in the stock. Your portfolio tracking system should be based on what you pay for stock, and not on how price changes occur from one day to the next. If your basis in the stock is $15 per share, your net return will be much different from that of someone who paid $25 per share for the same stock.

KEY POINT: All calculations of return on investment (ROI) are properly based on what you paid for a stock, and never on how values change from one day to the next.

Earnings per share. Any numerical or financial information is meaningless without proper context. Even the basic earnings per share information you find every day is unreliable if it is not reflected in a realistic manner. Consider these two versions of the same fictitious information:

Version 1—Bad news

XYZ Corporation's latest quarterly earnings report was issued today. It showed earnings at 92 cents per share, up only one penny from the same period last year. Analysts expressed disappointment at XYZ's failure to improve upon its earnings, and share price on the market dropped by midday.

Version 2—Good news

XYZ Corporation's latest quarterly earnings report was issued today. It showed earnings at 92 cents per share, reflecting XYZ management's successful efforts to maintain earnings at an impressive 8 percent of gross sales for the period. In past periods, XYZ's earnings fluctuated in a broad range, adding to market uncertainty about the company. In reaction to the report, share price showed a midday drop caused by profit taking.

These short examples demonstrate how a slant can be put on financial news that affects investors' perceptions directly and significantly. Financial information is so complex that it demands proper interpretation by every investor. This is not as daunting a task as it might seem; it does not require a degree in finance, only the ability to interpret the raw material reported in the financial press in a way that makes sense. Determining the meaning of dividend yield and avoiding the distortions that result from the reporting of price point movement rather than percentage change are typical of the challenges that every investor faces. Finding information is relatively easy in these times of widespread access to the Internet. Information is exploding, and if anything, there is too much of it. Your task is to decide how to interpret what you find so that it provides useful information, rather than misleading information, about your stocks.

PUTTING THE LISTINGS TO WORK

In spite of the shortcomings of the daily stock listings, the information contained in them is valuable and revealing, as long as you are aware that it does not always present a reliable picture of what is happening. You should not simply take the information and use it without some judgment and adjustment.

Below is a summary of how the major pieces of information can be modified so that your information is accurate and reliable.

52-Week High and Low

The price trading range is an important piece of information that can help you make sound judgments about a stock's safety and stability. A narrow trading range implies relative safety and may indicate long-term growth potential if the trading range moves in an upward direction consistently over time. However, a "safe" stock may not offer the potential for enough price movement to interest you. It all depends on your definition of what constitutes a good investment, how much risk you are willing to take, and how long you plan to hold on to a stock.

The trading range of a stock also is an important technical test. Chartists believe that the trading range is defined by a resistance level on the top side and a support level at the low end. When a stock's price tests resistance and support by moving to the extreme high or low points of its range, chartists believe breakouts and readjustments to a new trading range may follow. Thus, the 52-week price range is important information for anyone following technical indicators.

> **KEY POINT:** Resistance and support define the trading range of stocks. The trading range is useful in predicting future price volatility.

A second use of the 52-week high and low is for evaluating volatility, the measurement of a stock's tendency to experience price change. Some people seek safe stocks with relatively narrow trading ranges; others are willing to pick highly volatile stocks with wide trading ranges, recognizing the potential for gain and accepting the risk of equally large losses.

Whether you use the trading range as a technical indicator or to test volatility, follow these guidelines:

1. *Use charts to identify what really happened.* In a 52-week period, a lot of price aberrations can take place. If a broad price range was caused by a one-time change that was a departure from an otherwise stable and narrow trading range, the 52-week range is unreliable. The exceptional price change, for example, could have been a reaction to an overall market price change and a subsequent correction. The most extreme points should be removed from your study.

2. *Use 52-week charts to distinguish between different price patterns.* Remember that a trading range can trend upward or downward. Where was the stock's price at the beginning and the end of the 52 weeks? Obviously, it means entirely different things if the stock is trading at or near its 52-week high or at or near its 52-week low.

3. *Consider price volatility as only one of many indicators.* Never choose or reject a particular stock only on the basis of volatility. It makes sense to review several important indicators to narrow the field of stocks under consideration or to identify possible changes to the

holdings in your portfolio. No single indicator should be used exclusively to make market decisions.

4. *Don't confuse price volatility with financial volatility.* Market price is a technical indicator that reflects the overall market's perception of value. A stock might be highly volatile in price for any number of reasons. Some corporations' levels of sales and profits each year are all over the board, with impressive net profits one quarter and unexpected net losses the next. But some companies with high levels of price volatility have very stable financial outcomes.

Price and financial condition are related to one another only indirectly. Price is a reflection of market perception about future profit potential, whereas financial outcome is only one of many factors affecting market price. A company's stock price tends to rise or fall based on perceptions in the market, even when the fundamentals have not changed. Among the most common reasons for this are:

- *Sectorwide perceptions.* A particular sector might be out of favor with investors, so that all corporations in that sector see downward trends in pricing, even though a specific company's fundamentals remain strong. A well-diversified corporation might not be affected that much by changes in its primary business, but the market perception may still drag down its stock price.
- *Marketwide pricing trends.* Extreme bull and bear markets have marketwide benefits or consequences. In a robust bull market, stock prices rise in general, often without rational support in the company's fundamentals. This creates a particular risk for investors, because ultimately prices will correct themselves, and stocks whose prices rise beyond reason are likely to fall more rapidly than average. When the market falls drastically, the same effect is seen on the downside. When a stock's price falls as part of a marketwide crash, it presents a real buying

opportunity, especially if the fundamentals do not correspond with the fall.

- *Popular trends and fads.* Some market sectors experience price changes without any logic whatsoever. Over the three-year period ending with the year 2000, the so-called dot-com companies (newly formed companies selling goods over the Internet) presented a market phenomenon seen from time to time—a new type of organization that captures the imagination of investors without any fundamental support. Many companies with no track record and often no profit experienced extraordinary run-ups in price. However, the run-ups eventually ended, and many inexperienced investors lost most of their paper profits.

Yield

The rate of dividend yield is too often overlooked by stock market investors. Instead, the emphasis tends to be on price movement, especially in the short-term. Even investors who intend to hold onto stocks for the long term may be easily distracted by short-term volatility in price, whether upward or downward in direction. But yield can represent the majority of overall return on investment.

KEY POINT: When studying long-term returns from stocks, don't overlook the importance of dividend yield. It is a significant part of total return.

Remember that the yield should be considered only in relation to the price you paid for shares. That will give you the true percentage yield you receive from dividends, and unlike a percentage based on current closing price, this percentage will change only when the corporation declares a different payment per share.

Consider entering into a program for reinvesting dividends in partial shares rather than taking dividend payments in cash. Many listed companies offer *DRIPs* (Dividend Reinvestment

Plans), which solve investors' problem of what to do with the relatively small amount of cash they receive four times per year. Direct purchase of odd lots is expensive; DRIPs enable shareholders to reinvest their dividends by purchasing partial shares.

> **KEY POINT:** You can search for companies with DRIP plans by using one of many free Web sites. One site to visit is *<www.dripwizard.com/dripinfo.asp>*.

Price change. The market as a whole is obsessed with daily price changes, and the financial press often gives half-hearted explanations for the changes:

> "The decline was caused by profit-taking."
> "Price consolidation was cited as the reason for the decline."
> "The upsurge reflected optimism among investors."
> "The surprisingly high earnings report was credited with the price gain on the day."

Certainly such factors will influence the price of stocks, but how significant is price change in the first place? Day-to-day change in a stock's market price is not at all significant when the larger picture is considered. Proponents of both major theories about the markets agree on one point: Short-term price change is unreliable as an indicator. It reflects daily adjustments and overreactions to news and rumor, and it should not be used for making market decisions.

> **KEY POINT:** Price change is interesting to shareholders and is emphasized in the news, but it reveals nothing of value for long-term investment decisions.

Even so, television, radio, and newspaper reports universally emphasize the largest price movements among stocks. Consumers of financial news must exercise great caution, because price change—and the way it is reported—is misleading and unreliable. For example, a four-point move in a stock selling at $80 is less severe than a one-point move in a $15 stock. The former represents a change of 5 percent, and the latter is a change of 6.7 percent. However, it is virtually certain that a daily news broadcast will highlight the four-point movement and fail to mention the less interesting one-point change.

You can use price movement information to accurately monitor your stocks. The change from day to day is unimportant, but the change in price compared to your original purchase price is the return on *your* investment.

In summary, using daily stock listings to monitor your stocks involves many pitfalls and opportunities to take information out of context. Your purpose should be to know what a particular type of information really shows, and to be able to use updated and changed information in a reliable and accurate manner. In most cases, information about things like exceptionally high volume or changes of dividend yield or price have little or no meaning for you. A study of volatility can be very misleading if it does not include study of the true nature of the price changes over a 52-week period. You also need to compare market volatility to fundamental volatility to determine how safe a stock's price is and how much you can depend on long-term financial strength to ensure growth in the stock's market value.

> **KEY POINT:** Too much emphasis on price volatility can distract you from the real information—the cause of the volatility. Sometimes a broad range is caused by atypical spikes in price.

Because current information tends to be price-oriented and does not address the real question of valuation and safety levels, when you use daily listings, you should modify the raw data so that it makes sense. If you are looking for long-term value, you may be keenly interested in current information at the time you buy shares, but after that, very little about the day-to-day changes in market price and volume will be revealing to you. The purpose in monitoring listings after you buy is to look for signs that long-term prospects or risk levels have changed. Market watching is one of the pleasures of owning stock, but it can be a mistake to take day-to-day changes too seriously.

PICKING THE BEST NEWS SOURCE

Which source of financial news serves your interests best? That depends on how much detail you need, and how often. It also depends on the kinds of investments you make.

For the investor who is holding only a few long-term stocks, a periodic review is sufficient. In this case, *Barron's* is useful because it provides a weekly summary in good detail, plus interesting news and opinion for the serious investor. *Barron's* also provides well-organized reports by market segment.

The more active investor, one who is likely to move in and out of market positions on a daily basis, will be more interested in the *Wall Street Journal* or *Investor's Business Daily*. These are also good sources for anyone who wants to read financial news from one day to the next. However, remember that even the daily papers are always a day behind. The serious daily investor needs to use the Internet for up-to-date stock prices and financial news.

For those who do not need a lot of detail, but just the highlights, *USA Today* provides a nice summary. The same is true for many metropolitan-area general newspapers that include a nicely detailed financial section.

The most up-to-date and comprehensive sources of information are on the Internet, where you can find both general news and specific information about individual companies. Some cable television news networks such as CNN, FOX, and CNBC, provide in-depth news and analysis, but unlike the Internet user, the television viewer has no choice about what information is covered. Chapter 8 provides guidelines for selecting useful television and radio financial news programs.

CHAPTER 4

Bond Market Listings

The universal regard for money is the one hopeful
fact in our civilization.

–George Bernard Shaw (*Major Barbara*, 1905)

Whereas shareholders own part of a corporation, bondholders loan money to a corporation or government agency.
The bond is the corporation or government agency's promise
to repay the money it has borrowed from the investor. The
word *bond* means commitment or promise.

Many investors understand the rules of the game for the
stock market better than those of the bond market. When you
buy stock, you own a small piece of a very large company; you
receive dividends, and if the company prospers, the stock rises
in value. If the company fails, the stock falls in value. It is very
straightforward. The bond market has a different set of rules
and characteristics. For example, well-rated bonds do not lose
their value as many stocks do. Shareholders are *equity investors,* bondholders are *debt investors.* The shareholder owns
part of the corporate whole, whereas the bondholder only
lends money to the company or agency, and the money is
repaid with interest.

Bondholders are protected by the corporation's contractual promise to repay bonds before stocks in the event of liquidation.

SCOPE OF THE BOND MARKET

While only corporations issue shares of stocks, there are three large classifications of bond issuers: the U.S. government, various government agencies, and corporations. The U.S. government funds its ongoing operations and the national debt through an array of debt instruments. The best-known instruments are Treasury bonds, Treasury bills, and Treasury notes. Government agencies that issue bonds include state and city municipalities and subdivisions. The bonds are set up to fund operations or to finance the construction of public infrastructure. Finally, corporations use bonds to finance operations. The interest on some bonds and other debt instruments is taxed, but interest on other instruments, such as municipal bonds, is tax-free. An interesting variation is the convertible bond. This is a debt instrument that can be changed into an equity instrument. The bondholder has the right to exchange the bond for stock at a contractual exchange rate. If the stock reaches a high enough price, it might be a smart move to convert the bond. Before converting, however, the bondholder should compare the bond's interest rate to the dividend rate being paid on the stock at the time conversion is possible.

KEY POINT: Risk levels establish how much interest a bond yields. The higher the risk, the higher the interest.

The competition among issuers for investment dollars helps to create market interest rates, which vary on the basis of bond safety ratings. U.S. government bonds, bills, and notes are secured by "the full faith and credit of the United States government," which is considered the highest possible safety guarantee for any debt instrument. Agency bonds may or may not be secured by one or more forms of promise. Revenue bonds include a safety feature tied to the estimated revenue that will be generated by the construction project for which the bonds were issued. If a city wants to build a sports stadium, for example, it might finance the project with revenue bonds, telling bondholders that the stadium's future revenues make their investment secure. Corporate bonds usually are secured by the net worth of the company, but some corporate instruments are intentionally unsecured. These instruments, called debentures, tend to yield higher rates than the safer, secured bonds. The security, or risk, of a bond establishes the level of interest that bond buyers can expect to earn. The safer and more secure the bond, the lower the interest rate; the lower the safety factor, the higher the interest rate.

Bond rating services set safety ratings based on the issuer's financial strength and history. The best-known rating system is that of Standard & Poor's, which defines corporate bonds in terms of the ability to repay. The four highest classifications are AAA (extremely strong), AA (very strong), A (strong), and BBB (adequate capacity to pay interest and repay principal). Bonds with ratings below these levels are not considered investment grade; they are predominantly speculative. Junk bonds, for example, are the lowest-rated—and highest-yielding—bonds.

KEY POINT: The term *investment grade* means just that. Buying bonds below investment grade entails too much risk for many long-term investors. The term *junk bond* also has a specific meaning: junk bonds have a higher likelihood of default.

THE VOCABULARY OF BONDS

Some definitions will help to clarify exactly what the bond listings reveal.

The *coupon* is the interest paid to the bondholder, most often twice per year. The *coupon rate* (also called the *nominal rate*) is the contractual interest rate.

The issue and maturity price of a bond is its *par* or *face value*–$1,000 in most cases. While the bond is on the market, however, its price can vary because its fixed coupon rate will be seen as more or less attractive as overall market interest rates change. For example, a bond that is issued with a 6 percent yield will become less valuable if future market rates rise above that level. Investors might be able to get 8 percent or 9 percent on other bonds, so the 6 percent bond falls out of favor. In such an instance, the bond's price will be discounted. So a $1,000 bond might sell at 97; this means that the bond can be bought or sold at $970 because it has a lower-than-market interest rate.

The same rule works in the other direction. If a bond is issued at 5 percent but market rates later fall below that level, the 5 percent becomes more attractive to investors. In this case, the bond will sell at a premium. So a $1,000 bond might cost you 103, meaning you have to pay $1,030 because you will receive better-than-market interest.

Current yield is a good indicator of a bond's current value. If a 5 percent bond is discounted to 97, its current yield is 5.15 percent (coupon rate divided by current price: $.05 \div 97$). If a 5 percent bond is selling at a premium of 103, current yield is 4.85 percent ($.05 \div 103$).

A final version of yield is called *yield to maturity*. This yield, which is a form of internal rate of return, is more complex to calculate. It takes into account the coupon rate and also calculates the discount or premium value between the current day and maturity. For example, if you buy a bond at a discount price of 97, the three points of the discount will be additional profit if you hold the bond to maturity. The extra profit over time is taken into account in the yield to maturity calculation. Likewise, a premium is deducted from the yield to calculate yield to maturity by the same process.

THE BOND LISTINGS

The major financial newspapers have special sections. The *Wall Street Journal, Barron's,* and *Investor's Business Daily* offer daily listings for several categories of bonds.

U.S. Treasury Instruments

The trade in U.S. government securities is a high-volume, big-dollar market. These debt securities fund the more than $5 trillion national debt as well as month-to-month government operating budgets. These are the safest of all debt instruments in terms of guarantee of interest payment and principal repayment.

> **KEY POINT:** You can learn more about trading U.S. government securities (including how to buy and sell online) and about the national debt at the public debt home page, *<www.publicdebt.treas.gov>.*

The U.S. government issues three major types of debt instruments. The longest-term of the three types are Treasury bonds. They mature in 10 years or more. Next are Treasury notes, which mature in 1 to 10 years. Investors can also trade in Treasury STRIPS; the acronym stands for Separate Trading of Registered Interest and Principal of Securities. The traditional Treasury bond or note has a specific number of interest payments over its lifetime; for example, a 20-year maturity will include 40 semiannual interest payments, plus repayment of the

$1,000 at the end of the 20 years. Investors in STRIPS buy only the right to repayment of the $1,000 principal, but they do not receive any of the interest. These zero-coupon bonds are sold at deep discounts from face value, because investors do not receive any interest. STRIPS are an appropriate investment if you want to ensure income in the future but you do not need interest payments in the meantime. STRIPS enable you to buy bonds at discount and, upon maturity, to be repaid at face value.

Treasury bills are the third type of Treasury securities. These mature in one year or less. They are reported in "days to maturity" rather than by maturity month or year.

Treasury securities are sold initially by auction, so interest rates are set by what dealers are willing to pay. The treasury competes with agencies, municipalities, and corporations for a finite amount of investment dollars. The treasury obviously wants to pay the lowest possible rate, and investors want to receive the highest possible rate, so the auction is an efficient way to set the price at which the federal government borrows money. Once the auction price has been established, high volumes of Treasury securities are traded over the counter among dealers and securities brokers, institutions, and individuals. A listing that is typical for Treasury bonds and notes is shown in Figure 4.1.

The six items of information shown in each listing are:

1. *Coupon rate.* The coupon rate is the annual interest to be paid to the holder of the bond or note. In the example shown in Figure 4.1, the $1,000 issue yields 5½ percent, or $55.00 per year, which will be paid in two semiannual installments of $27.50.
2. *Month and year of maturity.* The bond in the example will mature in February 2008. The *n* following the year means that this is a Treasury note. Treasury bonds have no designation following their year.
3. *Bid price.* The bid price is the highest price that bidders were willing to pay as of the end of the reported trading period. The price is expressed in percentage form. In

---

FIGURE 4.1   Government Bonds and Notes

The Wall Street Journal

| 5½ | Feb 08n | 96:21 | 96:23 | −8 | 6.05 |

---

the example, bidders were willing to pay 96.21 percent, or $962.10 for the $1,000-face-value note.

4. *Asked price.* The asked price is the lowest price at which dealers were willing to sell as of the end of trading for the reported day. In the example, this was $962.30 for the $1,000 note. The difference between bid price and asked price, or the *spread,* is the margin of profit that dealers realize when trading in Treasury securities. Although the margin often is quite small–.02 percent in the example–such trading is done in high volume each day.

5. *Change.* The change is the difference between bid prices for the close of the reported day and the previous day. This change is reported in basis points, so that the reported −8 means the bid price fell from 96:29 to 96:21.

6. *Asked yield.* This final column is the yield to maturity (YTM). In this case, YTM is 6.05 percent. This is a combination of the coupon rate and the difference between the discount and face value, spread out over the remaining time until maturity.

Listings for STRIPS, also called zero-coupon bonds, contain different information. A typical listing is shown in Figure 4.2. The six types of information shown in this listing are:

1. *Maturity.* The first column shows the month and year of maturity. In the example, maturity will take place in May 2012.

2. *Type of instrument.* This column contains a two-letter abbreviation distinguishing the type of STRIPS. In the

---

FIGURE 4.2   U.S. Treasury STRIPS

The Wall Street Journal					
May 12	ci	49:09	49:14	–7	6.08

---

example, *ci* indicates stripped coupon interest. Other abbreviations include *bp,* which means Treasury bond, stripped principal; and *np,* which means Treasury note, stripped principal.

3. *Bid price.* The bid price is the highest price that bidders would pay as of the end of the reported trading period. The price is expressed in percentage form. In the example, bidders were willing to pay 49.09 percent, or $490.90 for the $1,000 face value.

4. *Asked price.* The asked price is the lowest price at which dealers would sell as of the end of trading for the reported day. In the example, this was $491.40 for the $1,000 face value.

5. *Change.* This is the change in the asked price since the previous trading day, expressed in basis points. In the example, the change was -7, meaning that the asked price fell from a previous level of 49:21 to the current level of 49:14.

6. *Asked yield.* The yield to maturity (YTM) is based on the deep discount and the amount of time until maturity. To calculate the STRIP yield, the discount is spread over the period between the closing date and the maturity date. In the example, YTM is 6.08 percent.

Treasury bills are reported in terms of the number of days until maturity, because they will always mature within one year. A typical listing for a Treasury bill is shown in Figure 4.3.

FIGURE 4.3   Treasury Bill Listing

The Wall Street Journal

| May 31 '01 | 296 | 5.80 | 5.79 | +0.03 | 6.09 |

These six columns show:

1. *Maturity date.* The exact maturity day is given here. In the example, the bill matures on May 31, 2001.
2. *Days to maturity.* This is the number of days between the reported date and maturity. At the time of this example, August 8, 2000, there were 296 days remaining until the bill's maturity.
3. *Bid price.* This is the highest discounted rate that bidders would pay as of the end of the reported trading period. In the example, bidders were willing to pay 5.80 percent of face value.
4. *Asked price.* This is the lowest discounted rate at which dealers would sell as of the end of trading for the reported day. In the example, this was 5.79 percent of face value.
5. *Change.* This is the change in the asked price between the reported trading day and the previous day. In the example, the asked price fell 0.03 percent from 5.82 percent down to current level of 5.79 percent.
6. *Yield to maturity.* The last column reports yield to maturity. This is the yield based on the current asked price (today's discounted rate) and the number of days to maturity. In the example, yield to maturity is 6.09 percent.

Barron's reports the same Treasury securities information as the *Wall Street Journal,* but in a different sequence. *Barron's* reports bills first, then notes and bonds, then zero-coupons (STRIPS).

FIGURE 4.4   Government Agency Listing

The Wall Street Journal

GNMA Mtge. Issues

Rate	Mat.	Bid	Asked	Yld.
5.50	30Yr	89:20	89:22	7.14

Investor's Business Daily (IBD) also shows the same overall information but in a different sequence: stripped securities, bonds and notes, and Treasury bills. In addition, *IBD* attaches its own set of abbreviations to its listings:

n – Treasury note

a – stripped interest

b – Treasury bond, stripped principal

c – Treasury note, stripped principal

k – security on which no withholding tax is required for nonresident alien buyers

p – Treasury note on which no withholding tax is required for nonresident alien buyers

Other Government Debt Securities

Trading in U.S. government bonds, notes, and bills is a high-volume activity representing the majority of government-issued debt security trades. However, other agencies of the federal government also issue and trade bonds and other debt securities. The largest of these agencies include the Federal National Mortgage Association (FNMA, popularly called Fannie Mae), the Federal Home Loan Bank, the Government National Mortgage Association (GNMA, also known as Ginnie Mae), the Inter-American Development Bank, the Student Loan Marketing Association (SLMA, or Sallie Mae), the Tennessee Valley Authority, and the World Bank. A typical daily listing for a government agency is shown in Figure 4.4.

FIGURE 4.5   Muni Issues

Barron's

Issue	Coupon	Mat.	Price	YTM
Atlanta GA Airport	5.600	01-01-30	99¼	5.65

These five columns reveal the following information about the GNMA mortgage-backed security:

1. *Rate.* The nominal rate on this issue is 5.50 percent.
2. *Maturity.* This security has an overall 30-year maturity cycle.
3. *Bid.* The bid price was 89:20, meaning $892.00 for a face value of $1,000. This is the discounted current value that buyers were willing to pay at the end of trading.
4. *Asked.* The asked price was 89:22, or $892.20 per $1,000. This is the level at which sellers were willing to sell at the end of trading.
5. *Yield.* The yield to maturity is based on the asked price. In the example, the YTM was 7.14 percent, reflecting the combination of the nominal yield and the difference between asked price and face value at maturity.

The listings for this category of government securities is labeled "Government Agency and Similar Securities" in the *Wall Street Journal;* "Other Agency Securities" in *Barron's;* and "Misc. Debt Securities" in *Investor's Business Daily.* Listings in *IBD* show the change in bid level from previous day, whereas the other two sources do not.

Barron's shows additional information on a selection of muni bonds, the obligations of states, municipalities, and subdivisions. These bonds are exempt from federal tax and sometimes from local taxes as well. Figure 4.5 shows a typical municipal bond listing.

These five columns report the following:

1. *Issue.* This identifies the specific muni bond. In the example, the Atlanta airport bond is reported.
2. *Coupon.* The coupon is the stated, or nominal, yield of the bond, 5.6 percent in this case.
3. *Maturity.* This column reveals maturity date. In the example, the bond will mature on January 1, 2030.
4. *Price.* This is the current market price of the bond. The sample listing shows a discounted value of 99¼, or $992.50 per $1,000 of face value.
5. *Yield to maturity.* This is the current internal rate of return on the bond, including current yield plus discounted value (or less premium value) between the current date and maturity.

Corporate Bonds

A listed corporation may use both equity (stock) and debt (bonds) to raise money and fund its operations. When the ratio of debt to total capitalization is too high, that is seen as a negative sign for stockholders. The more debt a company carries, the more of its profits go to interest payments, so there is less left over for dividends or to fund further expansion.

KEY POINT: Corporations have to reduce dividends when they have to commit a growing proportion of profits to repaying interest, so astute investors judge long-term investments by studying the relationship between equity and debt capitalization.

Corporations issue many types of bonds with differing features, limitations, and advantages. Two important definitions will be helpful here.

FIGURE 4.6   NYSE Exchange Bond Listing

The Wall Street Journal and IBD

Bonds	Cur Yld	Vol.	Close	Net Chg.
ChaseM 6⅛ 08	6.7	5	91¾	+2¾

Maturity can mean the year the bondholder is repaid; it can also refer to the duration of the bond. A short-term bond matures in five years or less, intermediate-term bonds have a maturity of between five and ten years, and long-term bonds mature in more than ten years.

Security refers to the backing a bond has. There are numerous types of security. A mortgage bond is secured by real property owned by the company (plants and facilities, offices, land). Income bonds, also called adjustment bonds, are rare; the interest and repayment on these bonds is tied to the income stream of the company. Equipment trust certificates are used for the purchase of equipment; the company does not acquire title to the equipment until the certificate, or bond, is redeemed. Debentures are unsecured bonds; the promise to repay is based on the good faith of the corporation. Investment-grade debentures are only those with the best possible corporate rating—AAA or AA, for example.

The *Wall Street Journal* and *Investor's Business Daily* provide a sampling of bonds trading on the NYSE. A typical NYSE bond listing is shown in Figure 4.6.

These five columns report the following information:

1. *Issuer and bond.* This identifies the bond issuer, the coupon (nominal) rate, and the year of maturity. The listing in the example shows details for Chase Manhattan's bond yielding 6⅛ percent and maturing in 2008. The same issuer may have more than one bond, so the rate and year of maturity are part of the distinguishing information of the bond.

2. *Current yield.* This is the yield based on the current price—in other words, the yield you would be earning if you were to purchase the bond on the reported day. In the example, current yield is 6.7 percent. It is calculated by dividing the coupon yield of 6⅛ (the decimal equivalent is 6.125) by the current price of the bond (91.75, found in the second-to-last column).

3. *Volume.* This shows the number of $1,000 bonds traded on the reported day. In the example, five contracts were sold.

4. *Close.* The closing price of the bond often is at variance with the face value, or par value, of $1,000. In the example, the bond is selling currently at 91¾, meaning that you could purchase this $1,000 bond for $917.50.

5. *Net change.* The last column shows the net change from the previous day's closing price. The example shows that the bond was up 2¾ on the day, so the previous day's close was 89.

The weekly *Barron's* provides more detailed listings for a more extensive list of NYSE issues, in addition to AMEX issues and a handful of foreign bonds. It also provides a handy table of bond listing symbols. A typical bond listing in *Barron's* is shown in Figure 4.7.

This expanded listing summarizes a full week of activity in each bond. The expanded columns provide the following additional information:

1. and 2. *52-week high and low.* This shows the range of trading in the bond over the past year. In the example, the Chase bond traded between 86¼ on the low side and 96 on the high side.

6. and 7. *Weekly high and low.* The expanded listing shows the past week's trading range from low to high as well as the closing price. (The net change reflects the change from the previous week's price.)

FIGURE 4.7   NYSE Exchange Bond Listing

Barron's

| 52-Week | | Name and | Cur | Sales | Weekly | | | Net |
High	Low	Coupon	Yld	$1.000	High	Low	Last	Chg.
96	86¼	ChaseM 6⅛ 08	6.9	90	91½	89	89	−2½

Barron's offers another useful feature, a weekly "Market Laboratory" page for bonds. This summarizes the week's information in the overall bond market, including volume, statistics, mortgage-related securities rates, averages and indexes, a junk bond price-and-yield summary, an overseas bond index, and more.

Money Markets

Most investors are familiar with money market funds and accounts, which act like mutual funds but deal exclusively in short-term lending. Money market funds purchase and hold short-term debt instruments, like commercial paper (short-term unsecured promissory notes sold by financial institutions) or certificates of deposit, and they pay interest to investors on the basis of ever-changing market rates. Such funds are popular with investors, who deposit funds in them in the short term while awaiting other opportunities.

Each day, the *Wall Street Journal* summarizes money market status for short-term instruments in a narrative section that includes current prime rate, discount rate, and federal funds rates as well as brokerage call money rates and domestic and international rates on money market instruments of various kinds.

Summaries in *Barron's* are more extensive. They include top savings yields by institution, and they compare money market accounts and several classifications of certificates of deposit. *Barron's* also provides institutions' telephone numbers.

Investor's Business Daily's brief summary of money rates is arranged in sections according to classification and further subdivided according to differing rates for different numbers of days.

All three papers provide much more detail in listings for money market funds. Money market funds are the most popular avenue by which individuals invest in the money market; and for most people they are the only way to achieve any diversification. More information about money market funds is provided in Chapter 5.

EVALUATING BONDS

Bond listings provide an overview of interest rates and premium or discount levels, but for most investors, it is not the current price that reveals a bond's investment value, but the yield to maturity. Thus, YTM is the most reliable method for evaluating a bond's relative value.

> **KEY POINT:** Yield to maturity makes bond-to-bond comparisons valid, because the premium or discount is factored in. It is not accurate to compare bonds just on the basis of the nominal yield.

A bond's safety rating is equally important. A bond with a low safety rating will invariably offer a much higher interest rate; this is because the bond comes with a corresponding greater risk. You might earn significant returns investing in low-grade bonds, also called high-yield bonds or junk bonds, but preoccupation with interest rate alone is a mistake.

Selection of bond investments only on the basis of the financial listings is also a mistake, because the listings do not identify current ratings. Before buying bonds directly, it makes sense to investigate the issuer of the bonds. Of course, this step is not necessary for U.S. government securities, which have the best safety guarantee available; U.S. Treasury securities can be bought strictly on the basis of a comparison of rates and time until maturity. However, investors need to perform research before buying municipal and corporate bonds. The form of research varies depending on the specific bond. Brokerage firms that underwrite bond issues provide rating information, and subscribers to Standard & Poor's or Moody's have access to ratings for a wide range of issues.

Individuals interested in buying bonds are most likely to do so through an income mutual fund or balanced fund. Funds provide the lowest cost for purchasing bonds, as well as liquidity and diversification—all important features for managing your portfolio effectively.

KEY POINT: Income mutual funds provide the most practical and affordable method for most people to diversify a portfolio with a limited investment in bonds.

Whether you buy bonds directly or through a mutual fund, the important risk factors associated with bonds—factors that are not shown in the daily listings—define whether a particular bond issuer's rating fits with your personal risk profile. The obvious differences between investment-grade bonds and junk bonds are not the only aspect of market risk associated with bond investing. When you buy bonds, you also take a chance on future changes in interest rates.

Today's interest rates involve two components, and being aware of these components is essential when you are evaluating bond investments. First is the "real" rate of interest, which is controlled by the supply and demand of money and, to a degree, by Federal Reserve policies. Market rates reflect the supply of money in the market, and the demand for borrowed funds on the part of institutions, corporations, individuals, and the government itself. The second, less apparent component that affects interest rates is the expectation of inflation.

The greater the market perception that inflation will rise, the greater the effect on market rates.* When investors fear that inflation is on the rise, this fear has an effect on the market. Believing that rates will be higher in the near future, investors do not want to be locked in to today's rates. Conversely, if investors believe that rates will fall in the near future, they will want to buy bonds at today's rates and lock them in. Such perceptions have an effect on agencies and corporations depending heavily on debt capitalization.

This two-part pricing is the same as that for stocks. The current price of a share of stock is based in part on the fundamental strength of the company—on sales, profits, dividends, and so on. The second component of price is the multiple reflected in the PE ratio, which expresses the market's expectation about future value based on potential growth of the company and, consequently, of the stock's market price.

> **KEY POINT:** A study of bond yield and safety is only part of the analysis. You also need to question whether the bond's yield will be considered relatively high or low in the future.

Because the market for bonds—like the market for stocks—is based on projections, or estimates, of future value, current pricing of bonds will reflect the expectation of inflation and could be inaccurate. Bondholders take a significant risk because the interest rate at which they buy today might be low in comparison to market rates in the future.

---

*The two-part theory of interest rates was developed by Irving Fisher in *The Theory of Interest,* Macmillan, New York, 1930; and has been adopted and widely accepted as descriptive of how and why interest rates change.

Example–A currently-issued bond has a 20-year term until maturity. It yields 7½ percent, which is a relatively high rate by today's standards. You buy the bond. A few years later, market rates have increased overall, and comparable bonds are being issued that yield 9 percent or more. The 7½ percent rate is poor in comparison to the rates of other bonds, so the market discounts the value of your bond.

In the example above, you might decide to sell and replace your bond with a higher-yielding alternative. That is possible, of course, because the bond market is liquid and you will have no trouble selling bonds from your portfolio. However, because the interest rate is lower than market rates, you will have to accept a discount. In other words, your $1,000 bond may sell for much less because its fixed rate is low compared to current market rates. If you hold the bond until maturity, the full face value of $1,000 per bond will be repaid; however, you need to weigh the income you will lose by holding low-yielding bonds for the long term against the face value you will lose if you accept the discount.

On the other hand, a bond's interest rate could turn out to be relatively high. If you purchase a 7½ percent bond and market rates later fall below 5 percent, then you can sell the bond at a premium, because the 7½ percent rate is high in comparison to other available rates. As an investor, you will have to decide on two possible courses of action. You could sell the bond and profit from the premium value of the bond, but then you would have to reinvest the money at lower prevailing rates. Or you could hold the bond until maturity, meaning you would give up the premium value but enjoy interest income that is higher than going rates.

When you buy bonds, you may be committing capital for the long term and creating an illiquid situation, because if market interest rates rise, it may be impossible to redeem the bond investments before maturity without suffering a loss. So for bond investors, uncertainty about future market rates is a determining factor in deciding whether or how much to invest in debt securities.

Many formula investment plans suggest committing a portion of your portfolio to stocks and another portion to debt instruments. However, the percentage distribution probably does not reflect your individual investing goals or your risk-tolerance level. Rather than selecting a particular level of investment on the basis of an arbitrary formula, you should make your selection according to a specific goal.

> *Example*—You estimate that in 20 years you will want to have a monthly income stream, and you need to select an investment today that will help you achieve that goal. You are not willing to achieve this goal by investing in the stock market, because the uncertainty about market pricing is not a risk you are willing to carry. So you decide to invest in U.S. Treasury STRIPS because they have the greatest safety rating possible. They are sold at deep discount, and they accumulate value between purchase date and maturity, and you can select a STRIP that has the exact maturity date you desire. You will be choosing a particular type of bond to achieve a specific goal.

The financial news listings for the many types of bonds and other debt instruments provide essential basic information, but they do not provide you with everything that you need. For example, it is difficult to distinguish one type of bond from another. Some are *callable,* meaning that the issuer can redeem the bond earlier than maturity at its discretion. Other bonds are *convertible,* meaning that you can trade them for shares of stock if you wish. Some bonds are secured, and others are debentures. And of course, there is the all-important bond rating, which determines whether a bond is even investment grade.

You need the help of an underwriter or broker specializing in the bond market if you want to become involved directly in bond investing. The listings are a starting point; they are useful for making comparisons and for judging the relative health of equity and debt markets, but they don't tell you everything you need to know. Most investors who consider the purchase of bonds will conclude that the efficiency and ease of access of income mutual funds make them the most practical answer for investing in the complex bond market. Mutual fund listings are the topic of the next chapter.

KEY POINT: The newspaper listings are only a starting point in your analysis. To make an informed decision about which bonds to buy, you need much more information than the listings provide.

CHAPTER 5

Mutual Fund Listings

People want economy and they will pay any price to get it.

–Lee Iacocca *(New York Times,* October 13, 1974)

The holdings of mutual funds, or investment companies, account for a significant share of the overall market. As of late in the year 2000, mutual fund assets exceeded $7 trillion, and 60 percent of that was invested in stock funds.*

For many market investors seeking diversification and professional management, the low cost, ease of investment, and regular reporting of mutual funds makes them the most obvious low-maintenance choice. With mutual funds, investors can divide even a modest amount of capital between stock and bond funds, or between aggressive funds and conservative growth funds. Investors who do not want to buy stocks or bonds directly can find the support they need and want in mutual funds.

---

*Source: Investment Company Institute, September, 2000

> **KEY POINT:** For a statistical overview of general infor-
> mation about the mutual fund industry, review the Web
> site of the Investment Company Institute at <*www
> .ici.org*>

CHARGES ASSESSED BY FUNDS

Major financial papers' listings for the mutual fund industry
include numerous footnotes detailing the variations in fees.
Mutual fund fees include the following:

Front-end load. A front-end load is a sales charge paid by
investors; it would be more accurate to call it a commission for
the salesperson. About six out of ten mutual funds charge a
front-end load, deducting commission from the amount
invested. The maximum load allowed by the Securities and
Exchange Commission (SEC) is 8.5 percent. If you invest $100
in a front-end load fund with the maximum load, $8.50 will be
deducted, and only $91.50 will be placed into the fund. Many
funds charge not only for the original investment, but for subsequent investments as well. Some even assess the load against
reinvested earnings.

Back-end load. Owning shares in a mutual fund might be
significantly more expensive for investors who are assessed a
back-end load, a fee deducted when shares are sold, especially
if the value of the shares has grown substantially since the original investment. The back-end load, or deferred sales charge, is
one of the ways that funds try to hide the costs they assess to
investors.

12b-1 fees. One fee that is not as apparent as the load is the
so-called 12b-1 fee. Since 1980, mutual funds have been
allowed to charge a small percentage to investors to pay for

marketing and distribution expenses. The small 12b-1 fees, if added to a front-end or back-end load, can make mutual fund investing expensive, but many investors ignore the charge or are not aware that it might be deducted from their profits. Not all funds assess 12b-1 fees. Because they are nothing more than additional charges for marketing expenses, wise investors should not invest in funds charging 12b-1 fees.

Redemption fees. Some funds charge fees when investors remove funds from their accounts. They tend to be small and are assessed only if funds are taken out within the first few years after the account is opened.

Management fees. The professional managers of each mutual fund are compensated by way of a fee deducted from the fund's overall value. All mutual funds charge management fees, which cover payments to managers and staff, overhead expenses, and the cost of analyzing the market and individual stocks and bonds.

No-load funds. No-load funds do not assess a sales charge against funds deposited. However, like all funds they do charge a management fee, and some no-load funds charge a 12b-1 fee. Before selecting a no-load fund, be sure to check all fees, and make sure you understand exactly what costs are going to be involved. No-load funds differ from load funds in only one respect: no charges are taken from investment capital to pay a commission to a salesperson, so the full amount of the investment goes to work immediately.

Historically, load and no-load funds do not differ in market performance, so it makes no sense to have a commission deducted from your investment capital. Some people argue that the commission is worth paying because the salesperson can then guide them to the best possible fund; however, such claims cannot be established by performance comparisons.

No logic suggests that there would be a relationship between sales commission and market performance. The load pays the sales representative for bringing investment dollars into the fund. That individual has nothing to do with the investment decisions made by management. The astute investor avoids all funds charging loads, because loads are not necessary to achieve better market performance.

The daily mutual fund listings distinguish between the various configurations of load and other expenses with coded footnotes that are worth paying attention to. In addition, mutual funds should provide all potential investors with a prospectus, which investors should study thoroughly so that they know all of the fees and costs in advance and can make comparisons between funds.

> **KEY POINT:** The Investment Company Institute includes links to all of its member mutual funds on its Web site at *<www.ici.org>*. At a mutual fund's site you can request a prospectus, and sometimes even download one directly.

The daily listings do not tell the whole story of the costs of buying mutual fund shares. It would not be reasonable to expect all of the possible variations on fee types and levels to be included. Before you select a mutual fund investment, you need to review the prospectus and determine the level of every kind of fee involved. If you invest in a load fund, you may have to pay sales commission each and every time you invest. But there is no need to pay loads if you are making your own decisions.

OPEN-END MUTUAL FUNDS

Open-end mutual funds, those that sell shares to all buyers without limitation, are the best-known and most popular types of funds. In the financial papers, they are listed alphabetically,

---

FIGURE 5.1   Mutual Fund Listings

The Wall Street Journal

NAME	NAV	NET CHG	YLD % RET
Evergreen Select			
AdjRtel p	9.52	–0.01	+3.9
CorEqtl	90.78	+0.99	+1.3
CorEqtlS p	84.48	+0.92	+1.2
FixIncl	5.79	–0.01	+4.9
FixIncll	12.23	–0.01	+5.0

---

with subdivisions for specific funds within families of funds. Most fund listings share a shortcoming with individual stock listings: yields are not related to your purchase date. The *Wall Street Journal* reports only year-to-date yield in its daily listings. This is useful if you are comparing one fund's current year performance to that of another, but it is not of much help in tracking your own investment dollars. Furthermore, returns are presented on the assumption that all earnings would be reinvested. For individuals taking earnings in cash, the rate of return is much different.

The *Wall Street Journal* reports mutual funds as shown in Figure 5.1.

This partial listing shows the following for part of the Evergreen Select family of funds:

1. *Name.* The family of funds and specific funds within that family are named, and are footnoted when necessary. This example shows the first five funds in the Evergreen Select family. The letter *p* after the first and third funds indicates that these funds charge 12b-1 fees. Other important designations include *r* (redemption fee applies) and *t* (sales charges, or load, applies). None of the funds in this example assess loads or redemption fees.
2. *Net asset value.* The net asset value per share (NAV) is reported for each fund in the next column. NAV is derived

by dividing the equity value of the fund (total assets less liabilities) by the fund's number of shares outstanding. The result is expressed in dollars and cents.

3. *Net change.* This column shows the net change in NAV since the previous business day.

4. *Yield.* This is the year-to-date return, or a summary of increase or decrease in NAV since the beginning of the calendar year.

KEY POINT: Mutual fund listings similar to the *Wall Street Journal* listings are provided daily in *USA Today*. To review updated market information online, check the *USA Today* financial page at *<markets.usatoday .com>*.

The *Wall Street Journal* supplements its detailed mutual fund listings with more than 100 online Mutual Fund Scoreboards. There are scoreboards for the 10 biggest funds, the past year's top performers, and the past year's worst performers. The scoreboards are exceptional at-a-glance overviews of fund performance. A typical listing scoreboard is shown in Figure 5.2.

The scoreboard shows for each listed fund:

1. *Name.* Each fund included on the qualifying list is identified. Three samples are shown in the category of *A*-or-better-rated corporate debt funds.

2. *Total return, current year.* This is the return for the current year only, January 1 to August 4, 2000, in the example.

3., 4., and 5. *Total return for one, three, and five years.* These columns show the returns that were earned over the three periods identified, revealing the degree of consistency the funds were able to achieve.

FIGURE 5.2   Mutual Fund Scoreboard

The Wall Street Journal

Corporate Debt, A-Rated (funds investing at least 65 percent of assets in corporate debts rated "A" or better)

10 BIGGEST FUNDS

Total Return for Period Ended Aug. 4

FUND NAME	Since 12/31	1 Year	3 Years	5 Years	Assets (millions)	Phone Number
Bond Fund of America	3.2%	5.0%	4.6%	6.6%	$9,096.5	800-421-4120
Vanguard Lg.-Tm. Corp.	5.8	5.9	4.9	6.7	3,578.8	800-662-7447
T Rowe Price New Inc.	5.1	5.7	4.3	5.4	1,660.6	800-231-8432

6. *Assets.* The fund's total assets are shown in this column, allowing the investor to evaluate performance in comparison to the asset size of the fund.

7. *Phone number.* This is especially helpful information for investors desiring to contact the fund in the listing.

KEY POINT: The *Wall Street Journal* scoreboards are updated on a daily basis. To find and review them, log on to *<www.wsj.com>*.

Listings in the weekly paper *Barron's* provide substantially more information than the daily breakdowns in the *Wall Street Journal.* Included are all open-end mutual funds with at least $25 million in assets or 1,000 shareholders. A partial listing of funds as reported in *Barron's* is shown in Figure 5.3.

These 14 columns provide a wealth of information concerning trading range and historical rates of return: They are broken down as:

1. and 2. *52-week high and low.* the first two columns summarize the net asset value range for the last full year. This information, comparable to that provided for indi-

FIGURE 5.3   Mutual Fund Listings

Barron's

										LATEST DIVIDEND		
												12 MTH
52 Week		Fund	Week's		Close	Week's		% Return		Income +	Ex	Inc.	Cap.
High	Low	Name	High	Low	NAV	Chg.	1-Wk.	YTD	3-Yr.	Cap. Gains	Date	Divs.	Gain
		Sentinel Group:											
20.04	17.25	BalanA p	18.78	18.41	18.78	+0.39	+2.1	+4.6	+22.0	.153	6-22-00		.9454
20.07	17.27	BalanB t	18.82	18.45	18.82	+0.39	+2.1	+4.1	NA	.114	6-22-00	.466	.9454
6.05	5.63	BondA p	5.82	5.79	5.82	+0.03	+0.5	+3.2	+12.5	.036	7-23-00	.405	...
44.90	35.02	ComS A p	41.52	40.21	41.52	+1.35	+3.4	+5.0	+28.3	.062	6-22-00	.343	3.2191
44.81	34.94	ComS B t	41.40	40.10	41.40	+1.34	+3.3	+4.5	+25.2	.022+3.2191	12-16-9	.041	3.2191

vidual stocks, shows NAV history and enables you to see where current NAV resides in relation to the historical range.

3. *Fund name.* The example shows a segment of the Sentinel Group. Included are two classes of balanced funds, a bond fund, and two funds that invest in common stocks. The abbreviation *p* that appears after three of the five fund names indicates that 12b-1 fees are assessed. The abbreviation *t* that follows the other two fund names reveals that these funds assess both a 12b-1 fee *and* a back-end load. Other important abbreviations in *Barron's* are *n* (no sales commissions are charged) and *r* (redemption fees or back-end load are assessed).

4. and 5. *Week's high and low NAV.* This summarizes the current week's NAV range.

6. *Close NAV.* This is the net asset value for the fund at the end of the most recent trading day.

7. *Week's change.* The amount per share that the fund's NAV changed in the reported week, in dollars and cents.

8., 9., and 10. *Percentage return columns.* These three columns summarize the return earned on NAV for the reported week, the year to date, and for the past three years. This enables you to compare short-term and longer-term rates of return and to make comparisons between funds for the different periods.

FIGURE 5.4   A *Barron's* Scoreboard

The Week's Top 10

Fund	Investment Objective	One Week	Year-to-Date
World FDS: Thrd MI Russia	Emerging Markets	8.09%	4.26%
Lexington Trka Russia	Emerging Markets	6.55	18.25
UAM:Cambiar Oppty;Inst	Multi Cap Value	6.53	7.58
TCW Galileo:Value Opptys	Mid Cap Value	6.28	21.45
SS Research:Gl Res;A	Natural Resources	6.11	38.56

11. and 12. *Latest dividend, current week.* These columns show income plus capital gains and the ex-dividend date (the date on which shareholders of record earned the reported dividend). In the example given, only one of the listed funds reported a capital gain during the week.

13. and 14. *12-month dividend and capital gain.* These last columns summarize the dividends and capital gains reported by each fund for the last 12-month period.

In addition to its highly detailed listings for mutual funds, *Barron's* provides subscribers with a section devoted entirely to mutual fund news stories and financial reports. The "*Barron's* Mutual Funds" section includes scoreboards summarizing performance and results for the week's top 10, bottom 10, and largest 10 mutual funds. Part of a typical week's listing is shown in Figure 5.4.

These columns are self-explanatory. The one-week and year-to-date rates of return are particularly interesting because they provide side-by-side comparisons between immediate results and results for the year. The scoreboard report offers a nice overview of the best, worst, and largest funds on one page. The nearly 30 full pages of mutual fund listings in *Barron's* give you a weekly summary of the vital information about each listed fund.

FIGURE 5.5   Mutual Funds Listing

Investor's Business Daily

36 Mos. Performance Rating	Mutual Fund	YTD % Chg.	4 Wk. % Chg.	5 Yr. After- Tax Rtn.	Net Asset Value	NAV Chg.
Seligman Group $21.0 bil					800-221-2783	
D+	Commn Stk A m	–2	–2	+59	14.44	+.06
D	Commn Stk B b	–2	–2	—	14.36	+.06
D	Commn Stk D m	–2	–2	+54	14.37	+.06
E	CO MuniA	+7	+2	+14	7.04	—

Investor's Business Daily (IBD) mutual funds listings have some interesting variations in comparison to the listings in the *Wall Street Journal* and *Barron's*. A typical *IBD* listing is shown in Figure 5.5.

The information shown in the example reveals:

1. *36-month performance rating.* This feature helps you to see at a glance how a fund's performance compares to that of other funds. This moving rating includes all dividends and capital gains; each fund is listed according to its rating:

   A+ = top 5%
   A   = top 10%
   A– = top 15%
   B+ = top 20%
   B   = top 25%
   B– = top 30%
   C+ = top 35%
   C   = top 40%
   C– = top 45%
   D+ = top 50%
   D   = top 60%
   D– = top 70%
   E   = below 30%

The funds shown in the example were rated low in comparison to other mutual funds.

2. *Mutual Fund.* The four sample funds are part of the Seligman Group family of funds. Note that the bold-faced identification of the family of funds name is followed by total assets—$21 billion in the example—as well as the toll-free number. This is followed by the fund names and letters denoting fee status. In the example, two of the funds are followed by the letter *m*, which indicates that multiple fees are charged; and one is followed by the letter *b*, which means that 12b-1 fees are charged. Other important abbreviations include *n*, which means no initial load is charged (this appears after net asset value, the second-to-last column); and *r* indicates that redemption charges apply.

3. *YTD % change.* The year-to-date percentage change is the increase or decrease in net asset value since the beginning of the calendar year. In the example, the Seligman Group Common Stock A fund fell 2 percent in this classification.

4. *4-week change.* This is the percentage of increase or decrease in NAV over the past four weeks.

5. *5-year after-tax return.* This column shows the percentage increase or decrease in NAV over the past five years. When reviewed with the previous column, the information enables you to compare long-term performance with more recent performance. After-tax return assumes a 35 percent tax rate for dividend income and a 20 percent rate for capital gains.

6. *Net asset value.* The NAV as of the close of the day in dollars-and-cents value; note that when an *n* appears after the NAV, it indicates that no charges or fees apply to the fund.

7. *NAV change.* This is the dollars-and-cents value of change in NAV since the previous business day.

In its Tuesday and Thursday editions *IBD* also provides a detailed chart explaining how to read mutual fund listings. Another helpful feature is a table showing the leading funds for the past three years. The table includes a description of each fund's investment objective, its 10 largest holdings, its top new buys, and its top sells; and it provides bar charts comparing five years of performance of each fund to the S&P 500. A separate chart provides a summary of information for the top 25 growth funds, including name, percent change since specific market low and high dates, 36-month performance ranking, and net assets.

CLOSED-END FUNDS

Although the *Wall Street Journal* and *Investor's Business Daily* do not list closed-end funds, *Barron's* does have detailed weekly listings of them. Many daily papers in metropolitan areas also include partial or full listings.

A closed-end fund differs from the better-known open-end fund because it issues only a limited number of shares. The fund does not buy shares back from investors who wish to sell; rather, shares are traded on the stock exchanges. Listings are broken down by investment objective. Major categories include general equity funds, specialized equity funds, and income and preferred stock funds. Figure 5.6 shows a sample of listings from *Barron's*.

The closed-end listings report the following information:

1. *Fund name and trading symbol.* The listings are shown by name as well as by symbol. In the sample shown in Figure 5.6, the first five funds in the category general equity funds are included.
2. *Stock Exchange.* The abbreviation reveals the stock exchange on which shares of each fund are traded. The symbols for exchanges are *A* (American), *C* (Chicago), *N* (NYSE), *O* (Nasdaq), and *T* (Toronto). The symbol *Z* indicates that the fund does not trade on an exchange.

FIGURE 5.6   Closed-End Fund Listings

Barron's

Fund Name (Symbol)	Stock Exch.	NAV	Market Price	Prem. Disc.	52-Week Market Return
	General Equity Funds				
Adams Express (ADX)	N	43.35	37⅞	−12.6	42.0
Alliance All-Mkt (AMO)	N	46.75	42⁵⁄₁₆	− 9.5	31.5
Avalon Capital (MIST)	O	18.00	16	−11.1	− 7.2
Bergstrom Cap (BEM)	A	269.08	259⁵⁄₁₆	− 3.7	49.6
Blue Chip Value Fd (BLU)	N	8.28	8⁵⁄₁₆	+ 0.4	2.1

3. *NAV.* The net asset value of the fund is reported in dollars and cents.

4. *Market price.* The price per share is reported in this column. As of early 2001, prices were still listed in fractional values.

5. *Premium or discount.* The premium or discount is the percentage that market price trades above or below NAV. To calculate, subtract market price from NAV and divide the answer by NAV.

6. *52-week market return.* This is the fund's percentage yield (or loss, if preceded by a minus sign).

MONEY MARKET FUNDS

A specialized type of mutual fund deals only in the money market, which includes Treasury bills, time deposits, bank obligations, and commercial paper. *Barron's* includes a weekly listing of money market funds, divided into two major groups: taxable and tax-free funds.

A sample of money market fund listings is shown in Figure 5.7.

FIGURE 5.7 Money Market Fund Listings

Barron's

Money Market Fund	Net Assets (Mil. $)	Avg. Mat. Days	— Yield (%) — 7 Day	10 Day	7-Day Comp.
Bradford Money Fund k	2,348.2	30	5.94	5.96	6.12
Brenton US Govt MMF/Class S k	7.5	27	30	5.28	5.44
Brenton US Govt MMF/Trust Class k	36.3	27	5.53	5.51	5.68
Bunker Hill MMF	190.6	75	6.29	6.28	6.49
CG Cap Mkts/Govt Money Invmts r	262.1	30	5.96	5.95	6.14

The data included in the money market listings includes:

1. *Fund name.* The fund's name is provided in the first column. Note the one-letter abbreviations following all but one of the funds. The letter *k* indicates that all or part of the fund's expenses are waived. The letter *r* tells you that investment restrictions apply.
2. *Net assets.* This is the fund's dollar value, in millions of dollars.
3. *Average maturity in days.* Because money market instruments are short-term by nature, a fund's average days until maturity is important information to the investor, especially if interest rates are changing or are expected to change in the near future. In the sample, all but one of the funds have average maturity periods of 30 days or less.
4., 5., and 6. *Yield percentages.* Three columns are shown for yield. The first two are for the seven-day yield and the ten-day yield. The third column is for the seven-day compound yield, which is the fund's effective rate of return.

FIGURE 5.8   Variable Annuity Listings

Barron's

Fund Name	Unit Price	4-Wk. % Tot. Return	52-Wk. % Tot. Return
Pacific Life Ins.			
PACIFIC SELECT VARIABLE ANNUITY			
Aggr Equity	14.139	1.24	7.48
Bond & Income	15.588	1.38	5.27
Emerging Mkt	8.671	−8.01	4.88
Equity	30.222	−2.18	20.78
Equity Income	36.764	−0.19	1.90

KEY POINT: In addition to the detailed listings, *Barron's* provides free current yield rankings of money market funds on the Web site at *<www.imoneynet.com>*.

VARIABLE ANNUITIES

Variable annuities and variable life contracts are mutual funds with an additional feature: an annuity or life insurance benefit that is attached to the mutual fund investment. *Barron's* lists these products each week under variable annuities and variable life. A sample listing is in Figure 5.8.

The Variable Annuity information includes:

1. *Fund name.* Each fund is listed by name within the sponsor's subcategory. In this example, the sponsor is Pacific Life Insurance Company, and its product name is Pacific Select Variable Annuity. Within that product, numerous funds are established to achieve particular objectives. Investors are able to allocate their holdings

among the different funds and to transfer from one fund to another.

2. *Unit price.* This is the accumulated unit value. A unit is like a share; it represents ownership in a variable annuity or life contract.

3. *4-week total return.* This reports the yield over the past four weeks.

4. *52-week total return.* This is the yield over the past 52 weeks. The third and fourth columns allow you to compare between current yields to one-year historical yields. Both yield figures take into account the premiums for annuity or insurance that are a part of the overall contract.

PUTTING MUTUAL FUND LISTINGS TO WORK

Deciding on a mutual fund is a matter of comparison, and the means available for making that comparison are primarily historical. Most investors will consider six criteria before selecting one mutual fund over another, and it is good to know the assumptions behind each criterion.

Historical market performance. Investors want to know how a particular fund has performed over time, but historical information can be misleading. Fund managers like to promote a fund's record by using illustrations that are based on lump-sum investments made several years before. Much of the reported return is made up of compound returns on reinvested dividends; if the results of dividend reinvestment are removed, performance results might be substandard. For example, suppose you hear the following: "If you had invested $10,000 in the fund 30 years ago, it would be worth $43,219 today." While this might seem impressive, it represents only a 5 percent overall return, which is far below market averages.

It is instructive to review mutual fund performance in comparison not only to past markets in general, but also in comparison to *down* markets. How did the fund perform when the market was on a downward trend? Did it fall more slowly than the market as a whole? Or did it perform on a par with or even worse than the market? Historically most mutual funds performed *below* the market average. So the selection of one fund over another should be based on a study of performance in all kinds of market conditions.

Loads and other charges. The mix of load fees and charges can be complex and difficult to decipher. This is where daily listings in the major financial papers is helpful. Several consumer finance magazines also periodically publish special editions on mutual funds in which loads are compared among the major funds. This information is more helpful than what is disclosed in a mutual fund's prospectus, where information on fees may be hidden in the fine print.

There is no sound reason to pay front-end or back-end loads, 12b-1 fees, or redemption fees. Historically, no-load funds have performed on a par with funds that charge loads. Sometimes investors diligently seek out no-load funds, only to end up paying a 12b-1 fee without realizing it. Funds that charge a 12b-1 fee are asking their shareholders to pay for the cost of marketing the fund to yet more shareholders. This makes no sense. Seek out no-load funds that do not take out any redemption or marketing fees. That way, except the amount of the management fee that all funds charge, all of your capital can be invested.

Minimum investment requirements. Some funds require a substantial initial investment, and subsequent deposit levels vary from one fund to another. For a number of personal reasons, some investors prefer the funds with the greatest flexibility. An investor might prefer a fund that requires a $300 initial deposit and no minimum requirement after that over a fund that demands no less than $5,000 initially and subsequent deposits of $1,000 or more. But picking one fund over another just on the basis of investment minimum could be a mistake. The size of minimum deposits often is dictated by the investment objective and structure of the product, not by policy. For example, bond funds, unit investment trusts, and Ginnie Mae real estate pools may require a relatively large minimum because of the types of products in which they invest. Be aware, too, that sometimes flexible minimum-investment policies mask higher-than-average fees. Remember to look out for all types of fees, including the less obvious back-end load or redemption fees and 12b-1 charges.

Portfolio and investment objective of the fund. Another method for picking a fund is to review the stocks or bonds in which the fund's money is invested. Investors also consider recent rates of return and review the mix of holdings by sector. Funds often state an investment objective that describes broadly what the fund managers hope to achieve by choosing the companies they do. "Income" funds, for example, usually invest in bonds for interest or in stocks that pay higher-than-average dividends. "Aggressive growth" funds look for companies that have better-than-average longer-term growth prospects, but that also carry a higher degree of risk.

Finding a fund on the basis of its portfolio can be difficult, because most individuals will not be familiar with many of the companies listed, and that list of companies does not necessarily reveal whether a fund is a "good" versus a "bad" investment. Besides, the holdings of mutual funds are constantly changing, and it is hard to know how each holding contributes to the fund's market performance. Picking a fund by investment objective is also difficult. "Long-term growth" can mean entirely different things to different mutual funds. The selection of stocks or bonds that meet a particular stated objective varies between funds according to what each fund's management thinks at the time.

Asset size of the fund. Some investors believe that bigger is better, so they prefer investing in funds with hundreds of billions of dollars in assets, and they avoid funds with only a few million dollars. The question of size, of course, is more complex than that. Bigger is not always better. Some funds have such a large dollar value invested that it is difficult for them to move quickly in and out of markets or to make decisions based on momentary opportunities. And imagine the complexity of managing hundreds of billions of dollars. Some smaller, younger funds outperform the larger ones. Because some small mutual funds lack a long-term track record, it can be difficult to identify one that is well managed, but that does not mean that the larger funds are always better choices.

Scope of funds available within a family of funds. In a fund family with many different alternatives it is easy to move money around without changing companies. So many investors prefer fund families with multiple specialized funds. If you are saving for retirement with an IRA or similar instrument, investing in a family of funds makes a lot of sense. It is possible to divide a single account among several different funds on the basis of each fund's stated investment objective and to move cash between funds. However, be sure to select a family of funds that does not charge for the convenience of having a lot of choice. For individual investors, the convenience of a family of funds often is oversold. For example, moving your capital from an income fund to a growth fund in the same family might be no more convenient than moving the same money to an entirely different mutual fund.

KEY POINT: Mutual fund listings are like scorecards. Real research requires studying a prospectus and doing more digging.

Mutual fund listings provide a wealth of information concerning fees, making them a good starting point for picking a fund. By limiting your review only to those funds that do not charge loads and other fees, you will be able to identify a number of likely investment choices for which you can compare market performance over several periods, using both the daily or weekly listings and information from the fund's prospectuses. However, ignore the long-term results that funds like to publish. These provide you with no indication of likely future performance.

One of the problems with the standard mutual fund listing is excessive emphasis on return on NAV since the previous day, week, or year. The only return that is of significance to you as an investor is a comparison between today's NAV and the NAV at the time you purchased shares. And the NAV by itself provides only part of the picture. The return percentage is more meaningful because it includes the assumption that all dividends and capital gains were reinvested. So for purposes of comparing current performance to long-term performance, the various yields provide more information. NAV change is short-term and has no real meaning in terms of how *your* investment dollars are doing.

If you invest in mutual funds, it makes sense to track fund performance based on the timing of your own portfolio, but this becomes more complex when you make periodic additional deposits. If you place a lump sum in a mutual fund and reinvest dividends, it is fairly easy to calculate returns, because you have a single starting point. However, if you invest $1,000 and then add $100 per month, determining the rate of return is far more complex, requiring a separate calculation for each deposit with the fund. It might be easy to convince yourself that a fund is performing well when, in reality, the regularity of subsequent deposits is masking the true results.

Mutual fund investments can be a wise addition to your portfolio, especially if you diversify between funds and direct-purchase instruments, and between different objectives within the portion of your portfolio that is invested in mutual funds. Use daily and weekly listings to make comparisons, paying attention to those funds that consistently perform above the average. Consistent strong performance indicates a better-managed fund and greater likelihood of future returns above market averages. Avoid buying fund shares without thoroughly studying the fee structure and reviewing historical performance in all types of markets.

CHAPTER 6

Derivatives: Options and Futures

The greater the "risk," usually the worse the idea.

–Robert Heller (*The Super Managers,* 1984)

Some types of investments are far too complex or exotic for many investors; however, they might represent opportunities to enhance your overall portfolio. The daily and weekly press provides listings for options and futures—collectively called "derivatives." Derivatives can be purchased or sold. Investors who purchase derivatives are assuming a *long position.* This is similar to the position taken by purchasers of stock, where you are "long" when you are the buyer. However, in the case of derivatives, it is just as common to sell contracts, which is a *short position.* Sellers of options and futures enter into a sale transaction as the first step (also called "going short") and later close out the position with a "buy" order. The sequence is backwards. Most investors are far more familiar with the steps involved with taking a long position: buy, hold, and sell. When you go short, the sequence is sell, hold, and buy.

LISTED STOCK OPTIONS

The options market is highly specialized and complex. An options is an intangible right to buy or sell 100 shares of a particular stock at a fixed price and by a specified date in the near future, and it rises and falls in value according to price movement in its underlying stock. Options can be used in a variety of ways, some highly speculative and others very conservative.

Two aspects of options create their risk/opportunity profile: the time limitation and the valuation of the options. All options expire within a few months, so options investors expect the underlying stock to behave in the right manner. If you buy an option, you are hoping that the stock will move enough points in the desired direction so that your option becomes more valuable and can be sold at a profit. (You can also exercise your option by trading the 100 shares of stock at a fixed price that is advantageous to you.) If you sell an option, you are hoping that the stock will not move too many points, so that your sold option will lose value and can be closed at a profit. (A seller may be required to buy or sell 100 shares if the underlying stock's price goes in the wrong direction.)

> **KEY POINT:** Options have no tangible value; rather, their value rises or falls on the basis of price movement in the related, or underlying, stock.

The option's total market value includes so-called time value, which also affects the profitability of the investment. Time value evaporates over time, and with increasing rapidity as the expiration date approaches. For buyers of options, time value is a problem because it has to be offset by ever-rising value in order for the investor to earn a profit. For sellers of options, the evaporation of time value represents profit and is an advantage.

Options investors must make complex decisions based on whether the underlying stock's market value rises or falls. You need to comprehend the permutations of price movement before entering into the options market, and you also need to understand how time value affects the option's value. Options listings report the current premium value for the two types of options: calls (the right to buy 100 shares) and puts (the right to sell 100 shares). A shorthand description of an option includes the type of option (call or put); the expiration month; the value at which stock can be bought or sold, also called the striking price; the name of the underlying stock; and the current premium. When investors talk about a particular option, it is common practice to express all four of these terms in a single expression. For example, an "EK May 55 call at 6" is an Eastman Kodak call option that expires in May. The fixed striking price is $55 per share, and the current value of the option is $600.

> **KEY POINT:** The options market has its own lingo, a special set of terms unique to it. Options investors need to become familiar with this terminology; otherwise, it will seem like a foreign language.

The content and arrangement of options listings vary by newspaper.

The first classification of options, and the largest, is that of listed options—options on specific stock issues. Each listing reports all of the terms for the options shown in the paper each day.

> **KEY POINT:** The daily newspaper listings for options are not complete. However, the *Wall Street Journal* provides a complete summary each day of all listed options on its Web site at *<www.wsj.com>*.

The newspaper listings report relevant data for a selection of options on each stock. As of the publication of this book, options listings were still being reported in fractional values. Upon implementation of the decimalization program, options

FIGURE 6.1 Listed Options Quotation

The Wall Street Journal

Option/Strike		Exp.	Call Vol.	Call Last	Put Vol.	Put Last
DellCptr	37½	Aug	16	6	511	$\frac{7}{16}$
42^{11}⁄$_{16}$	40	Aug	793	3¾	1983	⅞
42^{11}⁄$_{16}$	42½	Aug	1604	2¾	470	1¾
42^{11}⁄$_{16}$	45	Aug	2011	1$\frac{1}{16}$	315	3¼
42^{11}⁄$_{16}$	47½	Aug	986	$\frac{9}{16}$	143	5⅛
42^{11}⁄$_{16}$	50	Aug	1020	$\frac{3}{16}$	196	7¼
42^{11}⁄$_{16}$	50	Sep	643	$\frac{13}{16}$	104	7⅝
42^{11}⁄$_{16}$	55	Aug	672	⅛	63	12½

will be reported in dollars and cents. A typical listing is shown in Figure 6.1.

This grouping reports the following information:

1. *Option.* The first column identifies the stock that under-lies the listed options. In the example, options are reported for Dell Computer. Beneath the name is the previous day's closing price for the stock. Dell closed the previous day at 42^{11}⁄$_{16}$.

2. *Strike price.* The next column reports the strike price for each of the options reported. The strike price is the dol-lar value at which options can be exercised. (For calls, it is the price at which 100 shares of stock can be bought; for puts, it is the fixed price at which 100 shares of stock may be sold.) In the example, strike prices range from 37½ up to 55, or $37.50 to $55.00 per share.

3. *Expiration.* This is the month during which the options expire. Expiration takes place following close on the third Friday in the month. In the sample, six of the op-tions reported expire in August, and one in September.

4. and 5. *Call option columns.* The next two columns report trading activity and closing price for calls, which are options to buy 100 shares of stock. Volume repre-

sents the actual number of trades for the day, and closing price is reported in dollars plus fractional values. For example, the first line reveals that 16 contracts were traded in the August 37½ call, which closed at 6 ($600). So if you were to buy this option, you would be required to pay $600 based on the previous day's close.

6. and 7. *Put option columns.* The last two columns report trading activity and closing price for puts, which are options to sell 100 shares of stock. In the figure's first line, 511 contracts were traded the previous day in the 37½ August put, which closed at ⁷/₁₆, or $43.75 per contract. To change the fractional value to a dollar amount, first calculate the decimal equivalent of the fraction by dividing the numerator by the denominator (7 ÷ 16 = 0.4375), then multiply the result by 100 (0.4375 × 100 = $43.75).

Listings in the weekly *Barron's* provide additional information on the most actively traded options, showing closing prices as of the week's end and volume for the entire week. A typical *Barron's* listed options quotation is shown in Figure 6.2.

The *Barron's* listing shows the following information:

1. *Company and exchange close.* The first column identifies the company whose underlying stock has the options and the exchange closing price at the end of the week. In the example, IBM closed at 115⅞; this closing price is listed in each column.
2. *Strike price.* The next column shows three different pieces of information. First is the expiration month, second is the strike price of each option, and third is the distinction between calls and puts. A call has no letter and a put option is identified with the letter *p* after the strike price. In the example, the first line reports information for a put that expires in August and has a strike price of 115.

FIGURE 6.2   Listed Options Quotation

Barron's

Company Exch. Close	Strike Price	Sales Vol.	Open Int.	Opt. Exch.	Week's High	Low	Last Price	Net Chg.
I B M	Aug 115 p	1676	10132	XC	6⅛	2⁵⁄₁₆	2⁵⁄₁₆	−3¹¹⁄₁₆
115⅞	Aug 115	6238	58020	XC	4	1¾	3½	+1⅛
115⅞	Sep 115 p	2447	4592	XC	7⅞	4⅞	5	—
115⅞	Sep 115	8829	33504	XC	7	4	6	+1
115⅞	Aug 120	9418	46644	XC	1¾	⅝	1⁵⁄₁₆	+ ⁵⁄₁₆

---

3. *Sales volume.* This column reports the number of options contracts traded during the week. In the example, the first line reveals that for the August 115 put 1,676 contracts were traded during the week.

4. *Open interest.* This column shows the total number of open contracts as of the end of the week. In the example, the first line reports that there are 10,132 open contracts on the IBM August 115 put.*

5. *Option exchange.* This is the exchange on which the option is traded. The abbreviation *XC* indicates that the options are traded on more than one exchange. Other abbreviations are *CB* (Chicago Board Options Exchange); *AM* (American Stock Exchange); *PB* (Philadelphia Stock Exchange); *PC* (Pacific Stock Exchange); and *NY* (New York Stock Exchange).

6. and 7. *Week's high and low premium.* The valuation of options is referred to as the premium. These two columns summarize the week's trading range by premium value. Trading in the IBM August 115 put ranged from a

---

*Open interest is the combination of long and short positions. In both cases, the Options Clearing Corporation takes the opposite side of the transaction. It acts as seller to all buyers, and as buyer to all sellers. The advantage to this is that it is not necessary to match buyers and sellers directly. However, you cannot tell from the number of contracts reported as open interest how the mix is divided between long and short positions.

FIGURE 6.3 Listed Options Quotation

		Investor's Business Daily				
Call (C) Put Strike (P) Price	**Vol.**	**Last Price**	**Vol.**	**Last Price**	**Vol.**	**Last Price**
	Aug.		**Sept.**		**Oct.**	
Merck & Co		Close 73¾				
c70	168	4½	8	5	45	6⅞
c75	1954	1½	185	2⁹⁄₁₆	373	4¼
p70	304	⅝	40	2	94	3⅞
p75	80	2¹¹⁄₁₆	74	3¾	4	5⅜

high of 6⅛ to a low of 2⁵⁄₁₆, or between $612.50 and $231.25.

8. *Last price.* This is the premium value at the end of the week. The first line shows that the IBM August 115 put closed at 2⁵⁄₁₆, or $231.25 per contract.

9. *Net change.* The last column shows the net change between the reported week's and the previous week's closing prices. The IBM August 115 put fell 3¹¹⁄₁₆, or $368.75 per contract.

In *Investor's Business Daily (IBD),* the reporting format is completely different from the format in the other two publications. A typical listing is summarized in Figure 6.3.

The *IBD* format divides columns by expiration month. The second and third columns show the expirations that will happen first. The listing in the example was taken from an edition early in August, so expirations for August and September were the next scheduled to arrive.

The fourth column shows the next expiration in the expiration cycle. Each stock lists options in a specific cycle; in the example, Merck has scheduled options expiring in January, April, July, and October; this is also called the JAJO cycle. The other two cycles are February, May, August, and November, or FMAN; and March, June, September, and December, or MJSD.

The *IBD* listings also show the company name and the closing price of the underlying stock on the first line. In the example, Merck's stock closed for the reported day at 73¾ per share, or $73.75.

In addition to this change, the listing also reports:

1. *Type of option and striking price.* The first column identifies whether the option is a call (*c*) or a put (*p*), and shows the striking price, or the price at which 100 shares of the stock can be bought or sold by owners of the option. In the example, the first line reports on the 70 calls (the calls with a striking price of 70).

2., 4., and 6. *Volume.* These columns show the number of option contracts traded on the previous business day. Note that there are three volume columns, one for each of the three expiration months reported. In the example, Merck 70 calls had volume totals of 168 contracts (August expirations); 8 contracts (September expirations); and 45 contracts (October expirations).

3., 5., and 7. *Last price.* These columns report the closing price for the previous business day. In the example, the Merck 70 calls closed the previous day at 4½ (August expiration), 5 (September expiration), and 6⅞ (October expiration). Dollar-value equivalents of these prices are $450.00, $500.00, and $687.50.

LEAPS

Listed stock options are the best-known form of options. However, two other types of options are listed as well. These are LEAPS and index options.

LEAPS (Long-term equity anticipation securities) are long-term options. The typical listed option expires within only a

---

FIGURE 6.4　LEAPS Listings

The Wall Street Journal

			Call		Put	
Option/Strike		Exp.	Vol.	Last	Vol.	Last
Microsoft	70	Jan 02	195	16	26	9¼
70	85	Jan 02	133	10½	—	—
70	90	Jan 02	137	8¾	—	—

---

few months, whereas LEAPS have much longer life spans, usually between two and three years. As expiration approaches, the LEAPS options roll into expiration for the month of May, June, or July, depending on the expiration cycle of the underlying stock's listed options.

LEAPS are reported in the *Wall Street Journal* as shown in Figure 6.4.

The *Wall Street Journal* listing reports the following information:

1. and 2. *Stock name and price and option.* The stock is identified by name, with the current price appearing in each row beneath. In the figure, Microsoft closed on the day at $70 per share. Strike price follows on each line. The example reports on LEAPS with striking prices between $70 and $90 per share.
3. *Expiration.* This column shows the options' expiration month and year. Each of the LEAPS options in the figure is scheduled to expire in January 2002.
4. and 5. *Call volume and last price.* These columns show the previous day's call volume and closing price. In the example, the first line reports that the Microsoft 70 call LEAPS option had 195 contracts and closed at 16, or $1,600 per contract.
6. and 7. *Put volume and last price.* The last two columns report volume and last price for each put, when applicable. In the example, only one put option is active, the

---

FIGURE 6.5   LEAPS Listings

Investor's Business Daily

Exp. Date	Strike Price	Volume	Last Price
Jan 02	25	14	22
Jan 02	40	36	12⅞
pJan 02	40	30	7
Jan 02	45	139	10⅝

Microsoft 70 that expires in January 2002. Its previous day's volume was 26 contracts, and it closed at 9¼, or $925 per contract.

Barron's reports each week's ending status for LEAPS in the same format it uses for listed options (see Figure 6.2). *Investor's Business Daily* reports LEAPS in the format shown in Figure 6.5.

This LEAPS listing reports:

1. *Expiration date.* Each company's LEAPS options are listed in order first of expiration date, then of strike price. In the example, four Dell Computer LEAPS options include three calls and one put, the latter identified by the letter *p* preceding the expiration date and year. All of the reported options expire in January 2002.
2. *Striking price.* This is the price at which each option can be exercised. In the example, the striking prices of the four options range from $25 per share to $45 per share.
3. *Volume.* This column reports the number of LEAPS contracts traded during the previous trading day. Activity in the January 02 put was 30 contracts on the previous day.
4. *Last price.* The last column reports the closing price or last reported price for each LEAPS option. The previous day's reported last price for the January 02 Dell Computer put was 7, or $700 per contract.

FIGURE 6.6 Index Options

The Wall Street Journal

Strike	Vol.	Last	Net Chg.	Open Int.
		DJ INDUS AVG (DJX)		
Sep 100c	33	$9\frac{3}{8}$	$+2\frac{1}{8}$	2194
Sep 100p	949	$\frac{3}{8}$	$-\frac{3}{16}$	7509
Dec 100c	2	$11\frac{3}{8}$	$+1\frac{1}{4}$	2373
Dec 100p	11	$1\frac{5}{8}$	$-\frac{13}{8}$	11214
Mar 102c	1	3	$-\frac{1}{8}$	83
Aug 102c	6	$6\frac{3}{4}$	$+1\frac{1}{8}$	68

INDEX OPTIONS

The financial press also reports on index options. An index option is based not on the stock of a specific corporation, but on one of several indexes. A listed stock option is related to the underlying stock on the basis of market price per share; an index option, however, is related to the underlying index on the basis of the degree to which the index's value varies from a base of zero. Investors who buy and sell index options are speculating on the movement of the index. The index moves and the index options change in value accordingly. Some of the better-known indexes in this group are the Dow Jones Industrial, Transportation, and Utility Averages; the S&P 500; the Nasdaq 100; the NYSE; the Russell 2000; and Value Line.

The *Wall Street Journal* reports trading in index options in the format shown in Figure 6.6.

This partial listing shows the following information:

1. *Month of expiration, strike price, and type of option.* The first column, labeled "Strike," reports three items of information: the month of expiration, the strike price, and the type of option involved. In the example, the first line shows information about the September 100*c* index

option. This is a call, and the strike price is 100, which translates to $10,000. The index involved is the Dow Jones Industrial Average. Puts are identified with a *p*.

2. *Volume.* This column shows the number of contracts traded for each index option. Volume was low in all of the sample options except the September 100 put, for which 949 contracts were traded.

3. *Last price.* This column reports the closing price of the index options. The September 100 call closed at 9⅜. This translates to a dollar value of $937.50 per contract.

4. *Net change.* This shows the change from the previous business day's close. In the case of the September 100 call, the option rose 2⅛, or $212.50 per contract.

5. *Open interest.* This is the number of open option contracts as of the close of business on the latest reported day. In the example, the September 100 call had open interest of 2,194 contracts. This information does not tell you how many contracts were bought and how many were sold.

The *Wall Street Journal* also publishes a useful summary of trading ranges for the underlying indexes on which index options are written. Figure 6.7 shows a partial report from the table, summarizing one day's trading activity in several underlying indexes.

This brief sample of listings from the table reports the following information:

1. *Name of the index.* The first column identifies the index and its symbol. For example, the symbol for the Dow Jones Industrial Average is DJX.

2., 3., and 4. *High, low, and close.* These three columns report the day's trading range and closing price. In the example, the Dow Jones Industrial Average ranged between 10,892 and 10,737, and closed at 10,867. (The DJIA index valuation is reported in hundreds.)

FIGURE 6.7 Ranges for Underlying Indexes

The Wall Street Journal

	High	Low	Close	Net Chg.	From Dec. 31	% Chg.
DJ Indus (DJX)	108.92	107.37	108.67	+0.99	− 6.30	− 5.5
DJ Trans (DTX)	289.82	287.78	289.42	+0.74	− 8.30	− 2.8
DJ Util (DUX)	354.04	346.15	354.04	+7.15	+70.68	+24.9
S&P 100 (OEX)	805.48	795.00	803.72	+7.87	+ 0.89	+ 1.4

---

5. *Net change.* This is the change in the index's value from the previous business day. In the example, the DJIA was up 0.99 points.

6. *Net change from December 31.* This is a summary of the year-to-date change from the previous year-end index level. The DJIA was down 6.30.

7. *Percent change.* This is the percentage of change from the year-end index level to the reported day's close. The DJIA was down 5.5 percent from the December 31 index level.

Listings of index options in *Barron's* provide additional information and summarize a week's activity rather than a single day's. The listings appear as shown in Figure 6.8.

These columns report the following information:

1. *Index name and closing level.* The first column is labeled "company" in conformity with stock listings even though indexes are named in the column. The exchange closing level is shown in each row beneath the index name. In the example, the Dow Jones Industrial Average closed the week at 10,768.

2. *Strike price.* This column shows three option terms: the expiration month, strike price, and type of option. The first row in the example reports on the August 105 call– the August call with a strike price of 10,500 on the DJIA).

FIGURE 6.8   Index Options

Barron's

Company Exch. Close	Strike Price	Sales Vol.	Open Int.	Opt. Exch	— Week's — High	Low	Last Price	Net Chg.
DJ Inds	Aug 105	134	351	CB	2⅞	1¹⁵⁄₁₆	2¾	+ ¾
107.68	Aug 106 p	1068	6836	CB	2¹⁄₁₆	¾	¾	−1½
107.68	Aug 106	926	9227	CB	2⁵⁄₁₆	1⁵⁄₁₆	2⁵⁄₁₆	+ ¾
107.68	Sep 106 p	508	7725	CB	3	1¾	1¾	−1½
107.68	Sep 106	472	4882	CB	3⅝	2¾	3½	+ ⅝
107.68	Aug 107 p	213	171	CB	1⅞	1⅛	1⅛	− ⁹⁄₁₆

Puts are differentiated by the letter *p* following expiration month and strike price.

3. *Sales volume.* This column reports the number of contracts traded in each of the index options. The August 105 call had 134 contracts traded during the week being reported.

4. *Open interest.* This shows the number of open contracts for each index option as of the close of Thursday's business (although the week ends on Friday, compiled totals are reported for Thursday).

5. *Option exchange.* This column shows the exchange on which the specific index option is traded. *CB* indicates Chicago Board Options Exchange. Other abbreviations are *AM* (American Stock Exchange), *PB* (Philadelphia Stock Exchange), *PC* (Pacific Stock Exchange), *NY* (New York Stock Exchange), and *XC* (composite).

6. and 7. *Week's high and low.* These columns report the range of premium value in each index option. For the reported week, the August 105 call ranged between a high of 2⅞ and a low of 1¹⁵⁄₁₆. Translated to dollars and cents, the option traded between $287.50 and $193.75.

8. *Last price.* This is the closing price for the week in each index option. The August 105 call closed at 2¾, or $275.00 per contract.

FIGURE 6.9   Index Options: Weekly Summary

Barron's

		Week's Range				Call	Open	Put	Open
	First	High	Low	Last	Chg.	Volume	Interest	Volume	Interest
CBOE DJ Ind Avg (DJX)	105.22	107.68	105.22	107.68	+ 2.57	12,356	183,583	14,130	226,185
CBOE DJ Tran Avg (DTX)	285.81	288.71	285.81	288.68	+11.73	38	681	8	333
CBOE DJ Util Avg (DUX)	325.47	346.89	327.47	346.89	+18.63	1	20	0	1

---

9. *Net change.* This is the change between the reported closing price and the previous week's closing price. The August 105 call was up ¾, or $75.00, for the week.

Barron's also summarizes the weekly activity in the stock indexes on which options are written, supplying breakdowns as shown in Figure 6.9.

This partial report shows the following information for each index:

1. *Exchange, index, and symbol.* The unlabeled column shows the exchange (Chicago Board Options Exchange in the example), the index (the sample information includes the Dow Jones Industrial, Transportation, and Utility Averages), and the trading symbol.

2., 3., 4., and 5. *Week's range.* These four columns report on the first, high, low, and last price. The first price is not necessarily the same as the previous week's closing price, because indexes and their components may open the week at a different level from the one at which they closed. In the example, the Dow Jones Industrial Average opened the week with a level of 105.22 (10,522), it ranged between 107.68 and 105.22 (10,768 and 10,522), and it closed at 107.68 (10,768).

6. *Change.* This is the point value change in each index for the week. In the example, the Dow Jones Industrial Average rose 2.57 points.

FIGURE 6.10 Index Options

Investor's Business Daily

Call (C) Put Strike (P) Price	Vol. Aug.	Last Price	Vol. Sept.	Last Price	Vol. Dec.	Last Price
DJInds		Close 105.70				
c106	232	1¹¹⁄₁₆	26	3¼	. . .	. . .
c107	9	1⁷⁄₁₆	. . .	. . .	. . .	. . .
c108	200	¾	1	1¾	. . .	. . .
p106	221	1½	130	2½	. . .	. . .
p108	1	3⅛	8	3½	. . .	. . .

7. *Call volume.* This is the number of call contracts traded on each index. The week's trading volume in calls on the DJIA was 12,356 contracts.

8. *Open interest.* This is the number of open contracts for all calls written on each index. There were 183,583 open calls at the end of the week on the Dow Jones Industrial Average.

9. *Put volume.* This shows the number of put contracts traded on each index. In the sample material, the week's trading volume in puts on the DJIA was 14,130 contracts.

10. *Open interest.* This is the number of open contracts for all puts written on each index. There were 226,185 open puts at the end of the week on the Dow Jones Industrial Average.

Listings for index options in *Investor's Business Daily* are reported as shown in Figure 6.10.

This information includes:

1. *Index name, type of option, and strike price.* The first column names the index, then reports whether the option is a call (*c*) or a put (*p*), and indicates the striking

price. In the example, the first row shows activity for the DJIA 106 call. The closing level for the week follows the boldfaced name of the index. In the example, the Dow Jones Industrial Average closed at 105.70 (10,570).

2. through 7. *Volume and last price.* There are three pairs of columns showing volume and last price. The first two are identified in boldface months, and the third is the next-arriving cyclical trading month. The last monthly expiration date is shown in the row with the index name, because it will vary by index. In the example, the August 106 call had a volume of 232 contracts and closed at $1^{11}/_{16}$. The September 106 call had volume of 26 contracts and closed at $3^{1}/_{4}$. There was no activity in the December contracts.

COMMODITY FUTURES

Commodity futures are agreements between buyers and sellers to trade a specified amount of a commodity in the future at an agreed-upon price. Futures are traded on a broad range of products, including agricultural goods, natural resources, and precious metals. A large segment of commodities is identified as the "financials": pricing in Treasury securities, Eurodollars, and foreign exchange. Depending on the products being bought and sold, measurements are made in tons, pounds, bushels, cents per gallon, dollars per barrel, or dollars per ounce.

The *Wall Street Journal* lists futures prices as shown in the partial listings in Figure 6.11.

This partial listing reflects the following information:

- *Identification of the commodity.* In this example, the broad classification is grains and oilseeds. The specific commodity is listed in bold print, along with the exchange where it is traded, the minimum trading unit, and the

---

FIGURE 6.11   Commodity Futures Prices

The Wall Street Journal

GRAINS AND OILSEEDS

	Open	High	Low	Settle	Change	Lifetime High	Low	Open Interest
CORN (CBT) 5,000 bu.; cents per bu.								
Sept	178¾	180	177½	177¾	1	265½	177	117,082
Nov	187½	187½	185¾	185¾	1¼	268½	185½	1,458
Dec	191	192½	189½	190	¾	279½	188¾	189,988

---

means of trading. In the example, the commodity is corn. It is traded on the Chicago Board of Trade (CBT), the minimum trading increment is 5,000 bushels, and valuation is shown in cents per bushel.

1. *Delivery month.* This unlabeled column reports the month in which a commodity is scheduled for delivery at the agreed-on price. The vast majority of sellers never intend to deliver a commodity at the price, nor buyers to take delivery. Trading in commodities is speculative and contracts are bought and sold on the basis of changing price levels. The delivery month reveals the time when the commodity would be delivered if the contract were not closed.

2. *Open.* This is the day's opening price. In the example, September corn was sold with an opening price of 178¾, or $1.7875 per bushel. The minimum standard contract is 5,000 bushels, the value of one trading unit would be $8,937.50 ($1.7875 × 5,000).

3. *High.* This column shows the high price for the day. In the example, September corn reached a high price level for the day of 180, or $1.80 per bushel.

4. *Low.* This column reports the lowest price on the day. September corn went for as low as 177½, or $1.775 per bushel.

5. *Settle.* The settled price is the price at which the last contract was written for the day in question. In the example, September corn closed at 177¾, or $1.7775 per bushel.

6. *Change.* This is the change from the previous day's settle price. In the example, September corn fell by one, or $.01 per bushel.

7. and 8. *Lifetime range.* This reports the trading range for all monthly deliveries since inception. September corn has traded between 265½ and 177, or $2.655 and $1.77 per bushel.

9. *Open interest.* This is the number of open contracts in the commodity for a specified delivery month. In the example, there were 117,082 open contracts in September corn.

Barron's reports weekly summaries for each commodity. An example of the *Barron's* format is provided in Figure 6.12. The listings include the following information:

• *Broad category.* This figure indicates that livestock and meat is the broad classification. The specific commodity is live cattle, and the futures trade on the Mid-America Commodity Exchange (MIDA) under the ticker symbol XL. The standard trading unit is 20,000 pounds, and value is listed by cents per pound.

1. and 2. *Season's high and low.* These columns report the high and low for the season, or the current cycle of delivery months. In the sample listing, the August contracts for live cattle have traded between 71.07 and 65.67, or $.7107 and $.6567 per pound. When multiplied by the standard contract level of 20,000 pounds, the trading range is between $14,214 ($.7107 × 20,000 = $14,214, $.6567 × 20,000 = $13,134) and $13,134.

3. *Month.* This is the delivery month for the commodity. The sample listings show delivery months of August, October, and December.

FIGURE 6.12   Commodity Futures

Barron's

Season's			Week's				Open
High	Low	Month	High	Low	Sett.	Chg.	Int.
			LIVESTOCK & MEAT				
Live Cattle						(MIDA TkrXL)	
20,000 lbs. — cents per lb.							
71.07	65.67	Aug	66.95	65.67	66.80	+.35	17
73.10	67.65	Oct	69.10	67.65	69.05	+.65	44
74.40	69.80	Dec	70.80	69.80	70.70	+.53	29

4., 5., and 6. *Week's high, low, and settle prices.* These three columns show the past week's trading range and last price. In the example, the August contracts' price ranged from a high of 66.95 to a low of 65.67, and the last trade was made at 66.80 cents per pound.

7. *Net change.* This shows the change in settlement price from the prior week. For example, the August live cattle contracts increased by 0.35 cents per pound.

8. *Open interest.* This is the number of open contracts in each commodity and for each delivery month. There were 17 open contracts in live cattle for the August delivery.

Commodity futures are listed in *Investor's Business Daily* as shown in Figure 6.13.

This breakdown includes the following information:

• *Broad category and commodity.* The broad category is shown first; in this figure, the listing is in the classification of oils, and the specific commodity is heating oil. The futures trade on the New York Mercantile Exchange (NYM). The trading unit is 42,000 gallons, and valuation is shown in cents per gallon.

FIGURE 6.13 Commodity Futures

Investor's Business Daily

Season			Open					
High	Low		Int.	Open	High	Low	Close	Chg.

OILS

HEATING OIL (NYM) — 42,000 gal., cents per gal.

High	Low		Int.	Open	High	Low	Close	Chg.
84.90	41.94	Sep	36,686	75.65	77.30	75.25	76.84	+1.19
85.00	46.49	Oct	21,836	76.25	77.45	75.70	77.07	+1.07
84.70	47.45	Nov	21,768	76.40	77.70	76.30	77.37	+1.02
84.20	47.67	Dec	25,137	76.80	77.90	76.60	77.57	+0.97

---

1. and 2. *Season high and low.* This is the trading range for the current season. In the example, the September delivery for heating oil traded between 84.90 cents per gallon and 41.94 cents per gallon. Based on the trading unit of 42,000 gallons, this translates to a price range between $35,658 ($.8490 × 42,000 = $35,658) and $17,614.80 ($.4194 × 42,000 = $17,614.80).

3. *Open interest.* The open interest column reports the number of open contracts for each commodity. In the example, there were 36,686 contracts open on the reported day for heating oil with a September delivery.

4. through 7. *Open, high, low, and close.* On the reported day, September heating oil contracts opened at 75.65 cents per gallon, went as high as 77.30 cents per gallon, went as low as 75.25 cents per gallon, and closed at 76.84 cents per gallon.

8. *Change.* This is the change from the previous day's close. In the example, September heating oil futures rose 1.19 cents per gallon.

The financial news sources use different symbols for the various exchanges. Figure 6.14 lists exchange symbols by news source.

FIGURE 6.14   Exchange Abbreviations

Exchange Name	Trading Symbol		
	WSJ	**Barron's**	**IBD**
Chicago Board of Trade	CBT	CBOT	CBOT
Chicago Mercantile Exchange	CME	CME	CME
Coffee, Sugar & Cocoa Exchange, New York	CSCE	CSCE	CSCE
Commodity Exchange, New York	CMX	COMX	CMX
International Monetary Market	IMM	IMM	IMM
Kansas City Board of Trade	KC	KCBT	KC
London International Financial Futures and Options Exchange	LIFFE	LIFF	LIFFE
MidAmerica Commodity Exchange	MCE	MIDA	MACE
Minneapolis Grain Exchange	MPLS	MGE	MPLS
New York Board of Trade	NYBT	NYBT	NYBT
New York Cotton Exchange	CTN	CTN	CTN
New York Futures Exchange	NYFE	NYFE	NYFE
New York Mercantile Exchange	NYM	NYMX	NYM
Winnipeg Commodity Exchange	WPG	WCE	WPG

FUTURES OPTIONS

Just as many stock market investors use listed options rather than investing directly in stocks, many commodities investors use futures options rather than placing on deposit large sums of money to take buy or sell positions in commodities. A futures option enables the individual to play the commodities market with only a small amount of capital at risk.

KEY POINT: Short sellers face significant risks in options and futures. This area is appropriate only for the most experienced speculators.

Options are available on a full range of agricultural, livestock, and metals futures, as well as on futures in the financial arena. Futures can be bought or sold on currency, interest rates, and agency notes. Like all options markets, this market

---

FIGURE 6.15   Futures Options Prices

The Wall Street Journal

AGRICULTURAL

CORN (CBT)

5,000 bu, cents per bu.

Strike Price	Calls-Settle			Puts-Settle		
	Sep	Nov	Dec	Sep	Nov	Dec
180	2⅜	10	14	4⅝	4	4⅛
200	¼	2¾	4½	22⅜	16¾	14¼
210	⅛	1½	2½	32¼	. . .	22⅛
190	½	5½	8⅛	12⅞	9½	8⅛

---

is highly speculative, and investors should enter it only with a thorough understanding of the risks involved.

Futures options prices are reported by the *Wall Street Journal* as shown in Figure 6.15.

This information shows:

- *Category of futures.* This example lists futures options on an agricultural commodity, corn, which is traded on the Chicago Board of Trade (CBT). The option trading increment is 5,000 bushels; each option relates to that amount of corn.

1. *Strike price.* This is the dollar cost per ton at which the option can be exercised. In the example, the first line reports on options with a strike price of 180 cents, or $1.80, per bushel.

2., 3., and 4. *Call settlements.* The next three columns report the last prices for the day on three groups of options: those expiring in September, November, and December. In the example, the corn 180 calls closed at 2⅜, 10, and 14 per contract, or $237.50, $1,000, and $1,400.

5., 6., and 7. *Put settlements.* The last three columns summarize closing prices for the day on puts expiring in

FIGURE 6.16   Futures Options Listings

Barron's

Month	Strike	Vol.	Open Int.	Week's High	Week's Low	Sett.	Pt. Chg.	Future Sett.
				CBOT				
Corn					5,000 bu.; cents per bu.			
Sep p	170	5453	6701	1¾	− ½	¾	− ½	178¾
Sep c	175	564	1281	8¼	5½	5⅞	−1⅞	178¾
Sep p	175	1088	1458	3½	1¾	2	− ½	178¾
Sep c	180	2407	2996	5	3	3¼	−1½	178¾
Sep p	180	2119	6231	6½	3¼	4⅜	− ⅜	178¾
Sep c	185	1795	2337	2¾	1⅝	1⅝	−1⅜	178¾

Total Call Volume 57,734   **Call Open Int.** 374,781
Total Put Volume 41,751   **Put Open Int.** 164,304

September, November, and December. The corn 180 puts closed at premiums of 4⅝, 4, and 4⅛, or $462.50, $400.00, and $412.50.

In *Barron's,* the weekly summary of futures options reports not by commodity, but by exchange. The exchanges include the Chicago Board of Trade (CBOT), Chicago Mercantile Exchange (CME), Commodity Exchange, New York (COMX), New York Board of Trade (NYBT), and New York Mercantile Exchange (NYMX). Each week's listings report information as shown in Figure 6.16.

These listings contain the following information:

- *Category and commodity information.* Arrangement of information in the *Barron's* listings is by exchange, so all CBOT-listed futures options appear under the same major heading. In the example, prices of corn futures options are shown as of the end of the reported week. Each option is based on a contract size of 5,000 bushels, and valuation is given as cents per bushel.

1. *Month.* This column shows the expiration month and distinguishes between calls (*c*) and puts (*p*).
2. *Strike.* This column shows the strike price in cents per pound. In the example, the first line reports a strike price of 170, which translates to $1.70 per bushel.
3. *Volume.* This column summarizes the number of contracts traded during the week. In the example, the first line reveals that the September 170 put traded 5,453 contracts.
4. *Open interest.* This is the number of open contracts at the end of the week in each option. The September 170 put had 6,701 open contracts.
5., 6., and 7. *Week's high, low, and settlement.* These three columns report the trading range (high and low) and the last price for the reported week. In the case of the September 170 put, trading ranged between 1¾ and ½ and closed at ¾, or between $175.00 and $50.00, closing at $75.00 per option.
8. *Point change.* This reports the change from the previous week as well as direction of the change. The option reported in the first line fell ½, or $50.00 per contract.
9. *Future settlement.* The last column shows the price at which the underlying commodity closed for the week. This enables investors to compare option values to the latest value of the commodity. Corn settlement was 178¾, or $1.7875 per bushel.

- *Call and put volume and open interest.* The two lines at the bottom of each listing section summarize activity according to total volume for the week and open interest. In the example, 57,734 calls were traded on corn options, and 374,781 call contracts were open. The volume for puts was 41,751, and 164,304 open put contracts were on the books.

Investor's Business Daily reports futures options each day as shown in Figure 6.17.

FIGURE 6.17   Futures Options Listings

Investor's Business Daily

CORN—5,000 bu.; cents per bu.

Strike		Calls			Puts	
Price	Sep	Nov	Dec	Sep	Nov	Dec
170	10.625	19.250	23.375	1.000	no tr	1.750
180	3.875	12.000	15.625	4.125	4.250	3.750
190	1.125	6.250	9.500	11.375	9.250	7.500

Prev. Day Call Vol. 11,861   Open Int. 370,889
(CBOT) Prev. Day Put Vol. 9,227   Open Int. 173,124

This listing reports:

- *Category and increments.* The first line shows the type of commodity and the trading increments. In the example, corn trades in increments of 5,000 bushels, and prices are reported in cents per bushel.

1. *Strike price.* The first column reports the strike price of the option. In the example, the first line reports on the corn options with a strike price of 170 cents, or $1.70, per bushel.

2., 3., and 4. *Calls.* The next three columns report the premium value for calls expiring in September, November, and December. The options premiums are reported in decimal value. In the example, the 170 calls closed at 10.625, 19.250, and 23.375. Fractional equivalents are 10⅝, 19¼, and 23⅜; and the corresponding dollar values are $1,062.50, $1,925.00 and $2,337.50.

5., 6., and 7. *Puts.* The last three columns summarize premium value for puts expiring in September, November, and December. The 170 puts closed at 1.000 for September and 1.750 for December (no trades occurred for the November puts). These decimal values are equivalent to fractional values of 1 and 1¾ and dollar values of $100.00 and $175.00.

- *Volume and open interest.* At the bottom of the listing, volume and open interest in calls and puts appear. Also shown is the exchange for each commodity. In the example, the previous day's call volume for corn was at 11,861 trades, and open contracts numbered 370,889; the previous day's put volume was 9,227 contracts, and open interest was 173,124 contracts. The trades took place on the Chicago Board of Trade.

The valuation increments and pricing methods of futures options are not uniform. Each commodity is reported in a different manner, so investors dealing in futures options need to ensure that they understand the pricing mechanism before they commit money to a trade.

Options on grains usually are reported in cents per bushel. So a price of 3850 translates to 38½ cents per bushel. This is multiplied by the number of bushels in each contract. If that number is 5,000, then the option's price would be $1,925.

Each option is valued using a different method, so the listings are exceptionally complex and difficult to understand. Becoming familiar with the listings requires study and observation. Like all investing, futures investing demands expertise before money can be committed wisely. In addition, potential investors should fully understand the risk factors of this highly specialized market.

KEY POINT: For a worthwhile summary of calculations of futures and options prices, check the online article, "Taking the Mystery Out of Points and Cents" at *<www .futuresguide.com/price.htm>*.

PUTTING DERIVATIVES LISTINGS TO WORK

The daily listings are much more essential to derivatives investors than to investors in stocks, bonds, or mutual funds. Options and futures are intangibles: their value depends on changes in underlying securities or commodities, they expire in the near future, and their value can change dramatically and rapidly.

The owner of stocks and bonds can afford to track investments only on a weekly or monthly basis, or even to perform reviews more casually. There are no deadlines, and there is no risk of significant loss as long as tangible value exists. Bondholders enjoy a contractual right, and stockholders are protected by the book value of the corporation and, for well-established companies, by the corporation's financial history and market strength. However, investors who speculate in options and futures depend on ever-changing daily listings to enable them to take advantage of momentary profits and to close positions to minimize unexpected losses.

> **KEY POINT:** The fast-changing nature of options and futures investing requires regular monitoring, not just weekly, but daily, and sometimes evenly hourly.

The newspaper listings for derivatives provide pricing value as of the end of each day. However, this news is invariably dated by the next day. It is essential for the serious derivatives investor to be online and able to check status using listings with only a 20-minute delay. The listings are available free of charge on many Web sites.

> **KEY POINT:** Free quotations for options are widely available on the Internet. Two sites that provide this service are CSFBdirect at *<www.csfbdirect.com>* and E*Trade at *<www.etrade.com>*.

FIGURE 6.18   Options Trading Symbols

Expiration Month			Striking Price			
Month	**Call**	**Put**		**Price levels**		**Symbol**
Jan	A	M	5	105	205	A
Feb	B	N	10	110	210	B
Mar	C	O	15	115	215	C
Apr	D	P	20	120	220	D
May	E	Q	25	125	225	E
Jun	F	R	30	130	230	F
Jul	G	S	35	135	235	G
Aug	H	T	40	140	240	H
Sep	I	U	45	145	245	I
Oct	J	V	50	150	250	J
Nov	K	W	55	155	255	K
Dec	L	X	60	160	260	L
			65	165	265	M
			70	170	270	N
			75	175	275	O
			80	180	280	P
			85	185	285	Q
			90	190	290	R
			95	195	295	S
			100	200	300	T
			7½	—	—	U
			12½	—	—	V
			17½	—	—	W
			22½	—	—	X

Every stock trades with a specific ticker symbol, but options have their own special abbreviations, which are added to the end of the stock symbol. This additional information contains two letters that identify the expiration month and the striking price. Figure 6.18 summarizes the trading symbols in use. This table is a handy tool, essential for obtaining quotations online.

For example, if a particular stock's ticker symbol is MOT, the proper identification of a July 55 call would be MOT.GK. The identifying letter for puts is different. A July 55 put would be identified as MOT.SK. Even though stocks can trade in a broad range, separation of the price ranges by 100 points is not a problem. It is unlikely that confusion will arise between options with striking prices based on stock trading at 55, 155, and 255 per share. The end-of-list half-dollar values arise as the result of stock splits. So a striking price of 15 would become 7½ after a stock split. The use of proper symbol abbreviations speeds up access to free quotations.

> **KEY POINT:** Trading rules and standards for options are summarized well by the Chicago Board Options Exchange (CBOE). The CBOE Web site is at *<www .cboe.com>*.

Futures trading is a highly specialized and complex form of investing. You must fully understand the trading rules, language, and unique risk factors of both futures and their derivatives, futures options, before investing money. Even the points and cents of each commodity are complex and difficult to understand. So you need to become familiar with the workings of this market before trusting the listings to guide you through the market maze.

The futures market also has an unfortunate history of abuse. Boiler room operators would set up phone banks and telephone people to try to convince them to invest in the futures market. Invariably, investors who responded lost all of their capital. The boiler room operators would close up and move once authorities began hearing complaints about their techniques. Many boiler rooms targeted elderly people and could wipe out a family's retirement savings with a single telephone call. Today boiler rooms are more dangerous than ever. They have increased their efficiency by combining telephone pressure calls and Internet strategies. Great caution is required before you invest any money in the futures market, only the most experienced and knowledgeable investors should place any capital there.

Also check the Web site of the Commodity Futures Trading Commission (CFTC), which is the federal regulatory agency

> **KEY POINT:** Two Web sites are essential for anyone involved with the futures market. National Futures Association (NFA) is a self-regulatory agency for the futures industry. You can use it to check membership and to obtain referrals. The NFA's toll-free telephone number is 800-572-9400, and its Web site is *<www.nfa.futures.org>*.

for the futures industry and the place to register complaints and investigate industry practices. The CFTC agency was created in 1974 to protect the investing public against manipulation and fraud in the futures business. The CFTC's brochure, called "Futures and Options: What You Should Know Before You Trade," is available by mail or online. It includes useful explanations plus addresses and contact numbers for all commodity exchanges. The CFTC's telephone number is 202-418-5000, and its Web site is *<www.cftc.gov>*.

Because options are so highly specialized, most investors are not actively involved in trading them, and some are willing only to put a small amount of capital at risk buying options now and then. With such a wide range of possible strategies, options trading can be high-risk or very conservative, depending on how and why they are used.

The futures market is similarly specialized, not only in terms of language and trading conventions, but also because of the fast-moving nature of the market and the high risks involved. The listings in financial papers do not provide an education about futures, but are only sources for information. The futures traders need to gain knowledge from sources other than listings and from direct experience; then they can use the listings to keep up with the market.

> **KEY POINT:** Listings do not educate investors, they only provide information. Understanding a market before investing is the essential first step.

Individuals can participate in the futures market, but the majority of futures contracts are bought and sold by commercial and institutional users of the related commodities. Speculators never own the commodity, and while they stand to earn exceptionally large profits, they also risk suffering exceptionally large losses. The special risks are aggravated by the complexity of the market and by the involvement of boiler room operations that take advantage of people by promising big, fast profits without disclosing the risk elements.

If you decide to invest in the futures market, you can do so through an individual account or through one of two types of brokers: a registered futures commission merchant or an introducing broker. You can also invest through a commodity pool, which works much like a mutual fund, combining the capital of many investors who own shares in the pool. All of these individuals or firms are required to provide you with a disclosure document before you make an investment. In addition, an essential requirement of futures trading is that you know who you are dealing with. Follow these guidelines:

1. Get more information than just what is available in the listings. Learn a market thoroughly before investing any money.
2. Never invest in futures on the basis of unsolicited telephone calls. You are certain to lose money by responding to a boiler room pitch.
3. Always insist on receiving a disclosure document before committing capital, and never allow anyone to pressure you to invest before you have read the risk disclosures. Understand the risks involved, and make sure you can afford them. Also be sure that you are aware of your contractual obligations when you purchase options or futures.
4. Know who you are dealing with. Never give funds to someone whom you have not checked out with the CFTC and the NFA in advance.

CHAPTER 7

Technical Indicators

When people are least sure, they are often most dogmatic.

–John Kenneth Galbraith (*The Great Crash 1929*, 1955)

A technical indicator is related to market prices. In comparison, a fundamental indicator is strictly financial. Although there is widespread respect for the fundamentals, most financial news is preoccupied with technical indicators: Today's stock prices are far more interesting than the company's financial strength–not necessarily more important in terms of analytical value, just more interesting.

THE INDEXES AND AVERAGES

The financial press provides a highly detailed array of tables about indexes and averages, overall prices, advancing and declining issues, biggest rising and falling stocks, and dozens of other pieces of statistical information. The challenge to every investor is to figure out what forms of technical information–if any–are useful for monitoring an individual portfolio.

Stock market analysis is dominated by a preoccupation with indexes. Investors study, analyze, and predict the temperature or mood of the market on the basis of price movement of certain averages, to the extent that a particular collection of stocks becomes the market in the minds of the majority of investors.

> **KEY POINT:** It's the nature of the market to monitor by way of broad indexes and averages. However, all such indexes are flawed by their very nature. For those interested in tracking only a few stocks, the value of indexes is limited.

The best-known among these averages is the Dow Jones Industrial Average (DJIA). This is an index of 30 stocks of some of the largest U.S. corporations, which represent about one-fifth of the total U.S. stock market in terms of sales and profits. Changes in the DJIA are reported in virtually all financial news sources, in newspapers and online, on radio and on television.

In addition to the industrial averages, Dow Jones & Company also reports the entire U.S. market in the less-known Dow Jones U.S. Total Market index, the Dow Jones Utility Average, and the Dow Jones Transportation Average. The most reliable (and least watched) is the Dow Jones Composite Average, which reports overall price changes for all stocks.

Companies other than Dow Jones have developed their own methods of tracking the market. A close second to the DJIA in popularity is the Standard & Poor's 500. The S&P 500 is a far broader study of the market than the DJIA. It includes 500 stocks rather than 30, and it represents about three-quarters of the investment-grade stocks held by institutional investors such as mutual funds. Historically, the S&P 500 has tracked the overall market more accurately than the DJIA. The S&P 500 often is used as a basis for comparison. For example, when mutual fund performance is measured against the market as a whole, most often "the market" is the S&P 500.

The Nasdaq composite is a third popular index; it emphasizes technological issues. The Russell 2000 is another index cited in the financial press. It includes companies with market value between $20 million and $300 million, or about 9 percent of the total market.

TECHNICAL INDICATORS IN THE FINANCIAL PRESS

The financial reporting of the various measurements of price movement often is accomplished on a comparative basis. The financial press reports highly detailed information on market statistics overall and includes hour-by-hour breakdowns of index levels in some cases.

The Wall Street Journal

The *Wall Street Journal (WSJ)* compares the popular measurements of price movement in a daily summary in its "Market Diary" section. The section includes two charts that show monthly changes in the DJIA as well as changes during the past week. It also presents a series of statistical summaries as shown in Figure 7.1.

Each day's index or average is reported in this manner, making the tables useful for comparison. For example, note the differences between the point change of the DJIA (+99.26), the Total Market (+3.99), and the S&P 500 (+16.39). In addition to information on daily changes, this table also provides 12-month high and low and change in points, and changes since the end of the previous year.

The information in the summary report is supplemented by a more detailed daily breakdown called the "Stock Market Data Bank." The first section of the Data Bank contains a table that shows daily information for the major averages: the DJIA, the

---

FIGURE 7.1   Stock Index Summary Report

The Wall Street Journal

INDEX	CLOSE	NET CHNG	PCT CHNG	12-MO HIGH	12-MO LOW	12-MO CHNG	PCT	FROM 12/31	PCT
DJIA	10867.01	+99.26	+0.92	11722.98	9796.03	+ 159.31	+ 1.49	−630.11	−5.48
DJ US Total Market	344.16	+ 3.99	+1.17	364.71	285.95	+ 49.95	+16.98	+ 2.60	+0.76
S&P 500	1479.32	+16.39	+1.12	1527.46	1247.41	+ 181.52	+13.99	+ 10.07	+0.69
Nasdaq Comp.	3682.99	+75.63	+2.00	5048.62	2490.11	+1344.01	+53.36	−206.32	−5.07
Russell 2000	509.87	+ 6.25	+1.24	606.12	408.90	+ 83.98	+19.72	+365.12	+1.01

NYSE, the S&P 500, the Nasdaq, and others. It breaks down the following information for each index or average:

- 12-month high and low level for each index
- Daily high, low, and close
- Net percentage and point change for the day
- Net percentage and point change for the previous 12 months
- Net percentage and point change since the previous December 31 level

The Data Bank also reports the following:

- The most active issues on the three exchanges, the NYSE, Nasdaq, and AMEX, by name, volume, closing price, and point change
- Price percentage gainers on the three exchanges by name, volume, closing price, change in price since the previous day, and percentage of change
- Volume percentage leaders for the three exchanges by name, volume, closing price, point change, and percentage over each stock's 65 trading days' average
- Breakdown of trading volume in NYSE stocks by the half-hour

- Diaries for the three exchanges—this includes summaries for the reported day, the previous day, and the previous week, and shows:
  - Issues traded
  - Advances
  - Declines
  - Unchanged issues
  - New highs
  - New lows
  - Advance volume
  - Decline volume
  - Total volume
  - Closing tick (the net difference between stocks closing higher than the previous day and stocks closing lower)
  - Closing arms (a comparison between advance/decline and the volume of shares rising or falling, to measure relative buying or selling demand)
  - Block trades

This highly detailed statistical breakdown of the major technical changes for each trading day is quite useful. Investors and analysts who are tracking technical indicators that are tied to overall averages or to price movement and trends can use the Stock Market Data Bank to obtain most of the information they need.

The *WSJ* provides yet more. It summarizes the Dow Jones Industrial, Transportation, and Utilities averages in chart form for a six-month period and breaks down changes in the three averages plus a composite of 65 stocks (30 industrial, 20 transportation, and 15 utility stocks) hour by hour over the previous five days. In addition, a late-trading "Snapshot" reports activity that occurred between 4:00 and 6:35 PM, EST. Finally, the *WSJ* summarizes new 52-week high and low price levels for the NYSE, usually as a table within the NYSE Composite Transactions.

Barron's

Barron's also provides highly detailed information on a weekly basis, but in a different format from that used by the *Wall Street Journal.* Because *Barron's* is published weekly, it is able to provide a form of overview that would not be practical for the daily papers.

Averages are summarized in chart form for the DJIA, S&P 500, and Nasdaq composite. The charts are supplemented with a full-page "Winners and Losers" section, which includes 12 tables in four groups of 3 tables each:

1. Biggest percentage movers, both winners and losers, for the NYSE, AMEX and Nasdaq
2. NYSE most active, by volume percentage leaders, share volume, and dollar volume
3. AMEX most active, also by volume percentage leaders, share volume, and dollar volume
4. Nasdaq most active, by the same indicators

A partial table from the "Winners and Losers" page is shown in Figure 7.2.

This particular table reports only the largest price percentage change, but price change often is momentary and is subject to reversal of direction or correction, during trading days that follow the reported week. However, as a technical indicator, this table and the others on the "Winners and Losers" page is useful information.

The *Barron's* "Market Laboratory" page provides even greater detail for the week. Its seven pages include the following:

- Summarized 12-month weekly closes in the DJIA and cumulative daily breadth (daily advances minus daily declines, added to the following day's total to produce a weekly breadth level)

FIGURE 7.2   Winners and Losers Summary

Barron's

NYSE Biggest Percentage Movers

Winners

Name	Volume	Close	Change	% Chg.
BurnsIntSvc	98846	21³⁄₁₆	7¹⁵⁄₁₆	+59.9
AllpdPwr A	67827	4	1⁵⁄₁₆	+48.6
BeverlyEnt	44173	4⁷⁄₁₆	1⁷⁄₁₆	+47.9
Mascotech	30042	16¼	4¹¹⁄₁₆	+40.5
Entrade	8152	5¹⁵⁄₁₆	1¹¹⁄₁₆	+39.7

Losers

Name	Volume	Close	Change	% Chg.
KinamGoldpfB	951	9⁷⁄₁₆	−11¹⁵⁄₁₆	−55.9
CarmkeCnma	22500	2	− 1¹⁄₁₆	−34.7
Sport Supply	2184	3	− 1⁹⁄₁₆	−34.3
TrexCo	16469	39⅞	−16⅛	−28.8
Spherion	37757	12⅞	− 4¹⁵⁄₁₆	−27.7

- Half-hour index levels for the five days in the prior week, reported for the Dow Jones Industrial, Transportation, Utilities, and 65-Stock Averages
- A summary of the major indexes including weekly high and low, Friday's close and change, the weekly percentage change, the 12-month change and percentage, and the change plus percentage since the prior December 31
- A trading diary: advance/decline volume, advance/decline totals, composite daily breadth, AMEX composite, Nasdaq composite, and day-by-day numbers of advancing and declining issues
- A highly detailed page reporting specialty indexes, odd lot trading, initial public offerings (IPOs), stock volume, block transaction summary, and changes in the components of the Dow Jones averages
- U.S. Total Market industry groups, including major sector groups and subgroups, and for each, changes and ranking for the week and for the past 52 weeks

- SEC required filings during the week, a program-trading report, and an earnings scoreboard
- A two-page detailed listing of the Dow Jones Total Market Industry Group components, reporting broad classifications and listing the names of all corporations in each group
- Average technical indicators for stocks index-wide, including PE ratio, earnings yield, earnings in dollars, dividend yield, ratio of market value to book value per share, and dollar amount of book value; provided for the Dow Jones Industrial, Transportation, and Utility averages; and for the S&P 500 Index and the S&P Industrial Index
- Per-share value of stocks in the three major Dow Jones averages, provided by each company and including 52-week earnings and dividends plus book value
- The week's new high and low by name for the major exchanges
- Estimates of earnings for each company in the DJIA for a one-year period
- A summary of weekly high and low ranges of the Dow Jones averages, AMEX, and the Nasdaq
- IPOs and an equity financing summary for new issues
- Corporation name changes
- Trading suspensions

Investor's Business Daily

Like the other financial newspapers, *Investors Business Daily (IBD)* reports the Dow Jones Industrial Average in chart form. It shows not only point change and volume, but also summarizes the 30 companies of the DJIA for percentage change and volume range, and it reports volume and market change by the hour.

Smaller charts are included for leading sectors. These useful charts include a breakdown of the companies included in each sector index. *IBD* devotes less space than other papers to market statistics that are tied to broad point or volume movement, and more space to summaries of specific issues and industry groups. Some investors want broader reporting, but others choose the *IBD* approach of emphasizing individual stocks. It is a matter of individual preference.

Other Sources

Information about changes in the stock market averages are widely published in nonfinancial magazines and on radio and television shows. The next chapter includes useful guidelines for selecting television and radio programs for investment information. In addition, virtually every investment-related Web site includes daily summaries of stock market averages, including the DJIA, the S&P 500, and many others.

A Web search on any financial news or investment topic will lead to dozens of useful sites for gathering information about the averages. It is important, however, to recognize that stock market averages have both good and bad points.

Averages have value as generalized thermometers of the market. Anyone who has watched or listened to a financial news program knows that the market's condition is measured by movements in the DJIA or the S&P 500. Such reports are useful for gauging how investors view the market in general, and they may help you to time the purchase and sale of stocks, especially if you work as a contrarian. A contrarian believes that the best time to buy is when the market has fallen and most people are too afraid to put money in, and that the best time to sell is when everyone else is buying in a rising market.

On the other hand, the averages are only averages. They are not instructive for managing a limited portfolio of stocks, because they are intentionally broad. The averages do not indicate when you should buy, sell, or hold a particular stock, but they are useful for measuring overall market direction and sentiment.

Averages provide no information that you can use to time your personal investment decisions about specific stocks.

> **KEY POINT:** For detailed information about the most popular average, the DJIA, check the Web site at *<www.averages.dowjones.com>*. A listing of the companies in the S&P 500 is available at the Standard & Poor's Web site at *<www.spglobal.com/ssindexmain500text.html>*.

They are useful in making decisions only about the larger question of whether it is a good time to get into or out of the market. Trying to make decisions about individual stocks on the basis of movement in the larger averages is like trying to decide how an individual person feels about a question of social interest on the basis of a poll of thousands of people. While you can identify the average belief, you cannot know how any one individual stands on the question. The same is true in the market. Recognize that information in the averages is only a broad indicator. It is a mistake to attempt to use the averages for the timing of decisions about individual stocks.

OTHER TECHNICAL INDICATORS

There are dozens of widely used technical indicators. Among the most popular are the PE ratio, and data on odd lot investments, price changes and trends, and volume trends.

PE Ratio

The price-earnings ratio is a widely followed indicator that combines technical information (market price of a share of stock) with fundamental information (earnings per share). It is a comparative ratio indicating the market's perception of a stock's future potential. As a general rule, the higher the PE ratio, the more the market believes the stock has potential for price and earnings growth. The PE is expressed as a multiple of earnings per share.

One problem with the PE ratio is that historically lower-PE stocks have outperformed higher-PE stocks. So the market's immediate perception is often wrong, and an exceptionally high PE may, in fact, represent an overreaction to the stock's earnings potential.

A second problem is that while price is current information, earnings per share might be very dated. If the latest earnings report is three months old, how reliable is today's PE ratio? Because earnings per share might be vastly different today than it was at the time of the last report, PE is unreliable, especially for comparative purposes. If you compare PE over a range of stocks, some that have current earnings reports and some that have outdated reports, then the comparison is not valid.

KEY POINT: Before comparing PEs between different stocks, first check to determine how old the earnings per share is. The older the information, the less reliable.

Although the PE ratio is not a reliable tool for comparison, it can be used to track a stock's individual history, especially if you isolate your study to PE ratios that are calculated using prices that are posted within one month of their corresponding earnings reports. (Even with this limitation, it is important to remember that the corporation's accountants may adjust interim reports at the end of the corporation's fiscal year. The PE is one of many possible indicators, but its importance and value as a comparative financial indicator is overrated.

Odd Lot Trends

Technical investors follow odd lot trends in the belief that investors buying odd lots of stock are wrong more often than they are right, because experienced investors typically buy stocks in round lots. This is called the odd lot theory. Followers of this theory look for trends among odd lot buyers and sellers, and then take the contrarian view. For example, if odd lot

---

FIGURE 7.3   Odd Lot Trading

The Wall Street Journal

	Customer Purchases	Short Sales	Other Sales	Total Sales
August 4, 2000	4,459,359	363,407	6,052,148	6,415,555

---

investors begin selling shares—indicating that they believe the market is at a high and will fall—odd lot theorists take it as a sign that the market will rise. It is fair to say that investors who do not buy in round lots tend to be less experienced, but using any one indicator by itself is not advisable. You should track odd lot trends only as part of a larger program involving many other indicators as well.

> **KEY POINT:** The contrarian view is that odd lot buyers tend to be inexperienced, and thus are wrong more than they are right. Odd lot trends are convenient statistics for estimation, but they cannot be used as a sole means for timing market decisions.

Odd lot trading is reported in a brief table in the *Wall Street Journal* as shown in Figure 7.3. *Investor's Business Daily* does not report on odd lot trading on a daily basis.

This table reports the total number of shares traded on a specific day. Short sales are broken out because according to odd lot theory the short indicator is one of the most important statistics to watch. Short sales that increase in volume are a sign to the odd lot theorist that prices will rise, moving in a direction contrary to the expectations of the odd lot trader.

Every week *Barron's* provides a day-by-day summary of the previous five days of odd lot trading, as shown in Figure 7.4.

FIGURE 7.4   NYSE Odd Lot Trading

Barron's

Shares in Thousands

Daily	Jul 28	31	Aug 1	2	3
Purchases	4,410.5	6,200.0	5,308.5	5,238.5	5,989.3
Short, z	338,906	323,924	338,042	356,906	371,086
Other Sales	5,712.2	4,684.8	5,194.2	4,613.4	5,374.7
Total Sales	6,051.1	4,988.8	5,532.3	4,970.3	5,745.8
z-Actual Sales					

Price Trends

With investors' preoccupation with short-term changes in market price, it is not surprising that so much space in the financial papers is devoted to price information. The papers track advancing versus declining issues, biggest rising and falling stocks, and the number of new high and new low prices reached.

Advance/decline comparisons and new high/new low statistics are reported for all the major exchanges. A *Wall Street Journal* summary is shown in Figure 7.5.

Barron's shows each day's numbers in a table for the week as a whole. This is of greater use to most investors, because the one-week history is visible on a single table. An example of the *Barron's* weekly report is shown in Figure 7.6.

Investor's Business Daily does not report daily advances and declines, but it does provide a nicely detailed listing of stocks that have hit a 52-week new high or new low. A partial listing is shown in Figure 7.7.

This table subdivides the new high and now low issues by sector. In the example, the financial sector had 37 new highs on the day reported. The percentile ranking of EPS ratings is also helpful; for example, the stock in the first line had an EPS rating of 61, meaning that its earnings outperformed those of 61 percent of all issues traded.

FIGURE 7.5   Stock Pricing Trends

The Wall Street Journal

Diaries

NYSE	Mon	Fri	Wk Ago
Issues Traded	3,332	3,309	3,371
Advances	1,711	1,664	1,659
Declines	1,112	1,128	1,195
Unchanged	509	517	517
New Highs	117	99	81
New Lows	28	45	47

All of the financial papers devote a lot of space to comparing best-performing and worst-performing stocks in terms of percentage gains and losses for the day or week. Stock pricing information is short-term in nature, but a general shift of direction does imply a change in the market's mood. When the market is on a rising trend, more issues advance than decline, and when the market is falling, more issues decline than advance. It is questionable whether most investors need a table to inform them that the market is moving in a particular direction, however. Advance and decline trends are useful for market studies of a broad nature, but they are of little use on a day-by-day basis. The same argument applies to new high/new low statistics.

> **KEY POINT:** Price trends are interesting for studying the mood of the overall market. However, these data do not really help you to decide what to do in your portfolio. Your key questions—When do I buy? When do I sell?—are more complex, and the answers cannot be found in market-wide trends.

Price comparisons are of questionable value for most investors, those who are interested in longer-term price and earnings prospects for specific stocks.

FIGURE 7.6   Stock Pricing Trends

Barron's

NYSE Composite Daily Breadth

Daily	Jul 31	Aug 1	2	3	4
Issues Traded	3,371	3,327	3,337	3,324	3,309
Advances	1,659	1,643	1,557	1,300	1,664
Declines	1,195	1,215	1,311	1,535	1,128
Unchanged	517	469	469	489	517
New Highs	81	100	87	75	99
New Lows	47	37	37	58	45

Volume Trends

The major newspapers also devote a lot of space to volume trends, comparing block trades (trades by institutional investors) to overall market trends, and volume in rising stocks to volume in falling stocks. However, the study of volume is of questionable value to investors, because the significance of volume cannot be judged accurately. Every transaction involves a buyer and a seller, and the price at which a stock is traded is the price that both sides agree to. A general rule of thumb is that when a stock falls in price, its volume is being driven by sellers, and when the stock rises in price, its volume is being driven by buyers. However, in many cases, there is a mix of interests. As prices fall, bargain hunters pick up relatively cheap shares, and as prices rise, investors take their profits. So who is driving the volume?

KEY POINT: News summaries tend to oversimplify what has taken place in the market. They reduce information to numbers on tables and charts by necessity. The real information—and the most interesting—requires more digging.

FIGURE 7.7   52-Week High and Low Report

Investor's Business Daily

52-Week Highs & Lows
146 New Price Highs
159 New Price Lows

NYSE (n)—88 New Highs, 37 New Lows
Nasdaq—43 New Highs, 108 New Lows
AMEX (a)—15 New Highs, 14 New Lows

Name	Symbol New Highs	Price	EPS
Finance (37)			
GreatLkREIT (n)	GL	$18\frac{9}{16}$	61
SpiekrPpt (n)	SPK	$56\frac{9}{16}$	96
StifelFinancl (n)SF	$117\frac{7}{8}$	95	
VornadoRlty (n)	VNO	$40\frac{1}{4}$	68

Longer-term study of volume has greater significance. Many of the Web sites offering free charting services include both price and volume. When you study these two factors together over a one-year period, you will see that there is sometimes a relationship between volume and price. Over the past year, increases in volume might have taken place in advance of sharp price changes, so volume increases could act as a signal for similar changes in the future. Such an indicator is unreliable for important decision making, but it is another piece of information you might be able to use.

KEY POINT: Volume changes sometimes precede short-term price changes. However, history does not always repeat itself, and you have no way of knowing whether prices are going to change by going up or by going down; neither do you know when such changes will take place.

The significant influence of institutional investors, such as mutual funds, distorts factors such as volume. Funds may collectively own the majority of stock in many corporations, so significant volume changes can be caused by institutional decisions rather than by the decisions of individual investors.

CHARTING

Technicians are investors who emphasize price movement of stocks over the fundamentals. They recognize that financial information is largely historical, and they believe that nonfinancial indicators provide information of more immediate value. One major subgroup among technicians is the chartists. These are analysts and investors who study price patterns of stocks to predict near-term price changes.

In the past, investors who wanted stock charts needed to subscribe to specialized services or construct their own charts. This is a tedious procedure, especially if moving averages are to be involved. Effective charting requires the inclusion of detailed moving averages as well as daily or weekly price changes information. Now investors can access charts for specific stock issues free of charge on dozens of Web sites. A partial listing of free chart sites is presented in Figure 7.8.

Chartists point to past price patterns as proof that stock price movements are predictable, but hindsight is always better than foresight. Prices that moved in a consistent visual pattern in the past may not move in the same pattern in the future. Charting is not without merit, but the patterns charts reveal are dubious indicators if used by themselves and without consideration of other factors, both technical and fundamental.

You can learn a lot about stocks by comparing charts. A stock whose price has remained within a 10-point range over the past year is obviously less volatile than a stock whose price has ranged over 50 points or more. A comparison between an individual stock and the overall market trends also is useful,

---

FIGURE 7.8   Charting Web Sites

Bloomberg	<www.bloomberg.com>
Data Broadcasting Corporation	<www.dbc.com>
moneynet	<www.moneynet.com>
Quote.com	<www.quote.com>
Schwab	<www.schwab.com>
StockCharts.com	<stockcharts.com>
StockMaster.com	<www.stockmaster.com>
Wall Street City	<www.wallstreetcity.com>
Wall Street Research Net	<www.wsrn.com>
Yahoo	<quote.yahoo.com>
Zack's	<my.zacks.com>

---

because it can show how a stock's volatility is affected by the larger market.

To chartists, a *breakout* is a movement in price above resistance level or below support level. Support and resistance are the outer reaches of a stock's trading range. The lowest price in that range is called the support level, and the highest price is called the resistance level. Stocks tend to trade within these ranges until a breakout occurs, seen in price movement below support or above resistance levels. This movement may be temporary, or it could signal a new trend in the stock's price pattern. Chartists watch for a variety of patterns as signals that breakouts are going to occur. Among the more popular patterns is one that is said to indicate that a stock is testing support or resistance by approaching those levels and trying to break through.

The problem with charting is that it is based on the belief that price acts in a conscious manner. Market pricing is determined by ever-changing factors of supply and demand, which are fueled by rumor, gossip, and fact in a fast-moving mix. More often than not, pricing is driven by buyers and sellers who are overreacting to the large body of information that is forever flying about in the chaos of the market.

KEY POINT: A study of price patterns can reveal a lot about a stock's trading range. However, it is also important to make a distinction between serious analysis and market voodoo. Stock prices are not sentient, and placing too much importance on price patterns is misleading.

Charts for individual stocks, especially those that combine price with volume, are helpful to both prospective and current owners of those stocks. Charting Web sites provide periodic trading range information as well as moving averages. All of this information is available free of charge and can be updated as often as desired.

When combined with the study of other indicators, charting is useful for defining price volatility, for comparing pricing trends between stocks, for watching for bull or bear trends in a stock, and for identifying spikes that are not characteristic of the historical trading range. Moving averages are useful because they exclude the aberrations in daily or weekly price changes.

CHAPTER 8

Fundamental Indicators

The easiest job I have ever tackled in the world is that of making
money. It is, in fact, almost as easy as losing it. Almost, but not quite.

–H. L. Mencken (*Baltimore Evening Sun*, June 12, 1922)

The process of compiling and reporting financial news is
complex. Publicly listed companies are regulated by the Securities and Exchange Commission (SEC) and by state securities
agencies, and they are required to meet specific reporting
requirements and standards. They undergo periodic external
audits, conducted by accounting firms. These firms are
required to examine the books and records of the companies,
and to ensure that all reported information conforms to GAAP
(generally accepted accounting principles) standards.

Even with all of the oversight, however, corporations have a
lot of leeway in the methods by which they make their reports.
It is possible, for example, to defer some income to the following year and to take other steps to control the amount of sales
and profits being reported each year. For many stockholders of
large corporations, the regularity of earnings reporting is not
a problem. In fact, it has been observed that the CEO of a listed
company is responsible for ensuring that the stock's market

value holds and grows—and that this job is secondary to the more traditional role of a company's executives.

> **KEY POINT:** When fundamental information is reduced to a one-square-inch summary, it looks simple and straightforward. But the summary represents only the last step in a complex process. There is nothing simple about fundamental reporting.

The best way to hold a stock's market value steady is to consistently and reliably report earnings. If stockholders come to believe that they can depend on the company to report gradual and consistent growth in sales, dividends, and profits, then they will be confident that the stock's market value will grow steadily over time. The consistency and dependability of a company's earnings may form the foundation for the marketing strategy of larger stockholders, such as mutual funds. While a great deal of emphasis is placed on market price volatility, it often is more significant when a company demonstrates fundamental volatility as well. When fundamental, or financial, volatility is low (or under control), forecasting the rate of growth—in terms of sales, profits, dividends, and earnings per share—is relatively easy.

> **KEY POINT:** Accounting is not an exact science with only one answer to the questions about valuation and earnings. Audits are intended to ensure that standards are being followed, not to identify a single, unvarying right answer to those questions.

Financial reporting of earnings is far from perfect. Some believers in the fundamentals like to believe that accounting is a pure science because the books of the company are audited; in fact, there are many variables in accounting and auditing methods. To a degree, interpretations of some transactions are negotiated between management and the auditing firm. Latitude exists within accounting and legal guidelines. With a few exceptions, reporting of listed corporate earnings is more reliable today than it was in the past; and for the most part, the investing public can read financial reports with full confidence that the numbers are accurate and fair. That does not mean, however, that they are going to be interpreted correctly.

Even with the reliable information provided to the public, the analysis and interpretation of corporate earnings in the market remains in the Dark Ages. To some degree, analysts and investors do not understand the nature of corporate profits well enough to appreciate the significance of the major numbers. To a greater degree, the financial media impose unrealistic expectations upon listed companies, so that a very successful year often is reported as disappointing. Reporters, financial or otherwise, look for the simple message because they need to convey information to the reader in fairly simplified terms; this is a part of the problem because it leads, invariably, to oversimplification and lack of understanding in the press. In order to be accurate, fundamental information requires qualification and discussion with some depth. Some examples of misinterpretation are provided later in this chapter.

The oversimplification seen all too often involving fundamentals is typical of the problems associated with journalism. Because the interest is in capturing current news of interest, financial reports are prone to miss the significance of the bigger picture. In other words, how does today's fundamental status of a corporation affect long-term investment prospects?

There is a natural conflict between news reporting and long-term analysis. The news is ever-changing and the interest time span extremely limited. So all information, even the fundamentals, get reported in terms of today, this week, and this year. It is far less interesting (but significantly more important) to analyze the fundamentals with a view to the distant future. As a long-term investor, you are interested in determining how today's fundamentals affect your stock's long-term investment prospects.

In order to apply long-term criteria to the financial news, you need to take the information provided and interpret it for yourself. You cannot expect the financial news to provide this form of information for you. By its nature, the financial press must emphasize today's news. It cannot take on the role of the investor in trying to speculate about whether to hold or sell a stock. Some investors make the mistake of getting caught up in today's news and rumor and forget to perform the requisite long-term analysis—an understanding pitfall, but a serious one nonetheless. So you need to be aware of the dangers in paying too much attention to the news and too little attention to what that news means to you in terms of managing your portfolio.

CORPORATE EARNINGS

Each listed company is required to report its financial results every quarter and to issue an annual report containing a complete audited financial statement at the end of the year. The quarterly reports are reviewed for accuracy by an independent auditing firm, but not in as much detail as the year-end report.

Corporate reports of earnings are shown daily in the *Wall Street Journal* as illustrated in Figure 8.1.

This abbreviated earnings report provides the following information:

1. *Name and listing information.* The first line identifies the corporation, the exchange where its stock is traded, and its trading symbol. Playboy Enterprises is listed on the New York Stock Exchange, and it uses the ticker symbol PLAA.
2. *Reporting period.* The column headings in this line reveal the quarter and the reporting years. In the example, the quarter ends on June 30 and results are provided for the current year and the previous year.
3. *Revenues.* This row shows revenues for the quarter only, with the current year compared to the same quarter in the previous year.
4. *Net income.* The next line reports net income (sales minus costs and expenses). In the example, the current

---

FIGURE 8.1   Digest of Corporate Earnings Reports

The Wall Street Journal

PLAYBOY ENTERPRISES (N)		**PLAA**
Quar June 30:	2000	1999
Revenues . . .	$77,182,000	$77,759,000
Net income . . .	(5,883,000)	(2,972,000)
Avg Shares . . .	24,239,000	23,968,000
Shr earns:		
Net income . . .	(.24)	(.13)
6 months:		
Revenues . . .	150,285,000	151,143,000
aNet income . . .	(12,118,000)	(4,014,000)
Avg shares . . .	24,220,000	22,852,000
Shr earns:		
Net income . . .	(.50)	(.18)

a—Includes restructuring charges of $257,000 in 2000 and a gain of $1,728,000 from sale of an investment in 1999.

---

year's quarterly results show a loss of $5,883,000, compared to a loss in the previous year's quarter of $2,972.000.

5. *Average number of shares outstanding.* This line shows the number of shares outstanding for the period. The average is derived by comparing shares at the beginning and end of the quarter.

6. *Earnings per share.* This line shows the earnings per average share outstanding. In the example, the average share lost 24 cents this quarter, compared to a loss of 13 cents per share in the previous year's quarter. Earnings per share is computed by dividing net income (or loss) by the average number of shares outstanding.

$$-5,883,000 \div 24,239,000 = -.24$$
and
$$-2,972,000 \div 23,968,000 = -.13$$

(Note: Some calculations will vary due to rounding of reporting results.)

7. *Year-to-date results.* The next lines reveal the fiscal-year-to-date results. In the example, we see that 6 months have passed in the year-to-date, so we know that the reported quarter is the second quarter of the company's fiscal year. (Because fiscal years vary, it is useful to know whether results are for 3, 6, 9, or 12 months. Comparisons between the reported quarter and year-to-date results are valid only with this information.)

8. through 11. *Revenues, net income, average shares outstanding, and earnings per share.* The next four rows report identical information as that shown for the quarter, but the information is for the year to date. In the example, Playboy Enterprises reported fairly consistent results. Net losses for six months were approximately double those for three months, and the loss per share of stock for the quarter and for the year to date also were consistent.

12. *Footnote.* Any explanatory or qualifying notes are provided here. In the example, the footnote explains that the six-month reported net loss includes extraordinary items (those that will not be repeated) for both reported periods.

Barron's does not list all of the earnings reports for each week. However, it does provide two useful tables in a section called "Earnings Scoreboard." These tables include the week's major surprises and estimate changes. Surprises consist of the greatest variations between actual outcomes and the consensus estimates among industry analysts prior to the release of the earnings reports. Estimate changes consist of changes in opinion among analysts about upcoming earnings. The scoreboard is useful for investors who are looking for exceptional reports for the week, especially earnings surprises; however, the middle-of-the-road earnings reports are excluded from the summary. These tables show at a glance where significant changes have occurred. In comparison, a listing of the highly detailed earnings reports of all corporations reporting in a par-

---

FIGURE 8.2   Earnings Scoreboard

Barron's

Last Week's Major Surprises

Company	Period	Cons. Est.*	Actual Net Per Share
Positive			
Aurora Biosciences	2Q	0.05	0.19
Chiron Corp.	2Q	0.21	0.30
Career Educ	2Q	0.20	0.26
Negative			
Mercury Gen	2Q	0.56	0.47
Atwood Ocean	3Q	0.41	0.37
Berkeley (W.R.)	2Q	0.27	0.25

*Latest consensus estimate among industry analysts, as compiled by First Call/Thomson Financial (<www.firstcall.com>) before actual earnings were reported.

Last Week's Major Estimate Changes

Company	FY End	Prev. Fri. Cons.	Last* Fri. Cons.
Positive			
Internet.com	Dec.00	0.06	0.11
QLT Inc.	Dec.00	−0.29	−0.15
Martha Stewart	Dec.00	0.24	0.34
Negative			
Progenics Pharm	Dec.00	−0.26	−0.39
Netobjects	Sep.01	−0.21	−0.28
Gaylord Cont.	Sep.01	1.00	0.82

*Latest consensus estimate among industry analysts, as compiled by First Call/Thomson Financial (<www.firstcall.com>).

---

ticular week would require much more page space. Ultimately, investors need to look for information about their investments by making contact directly with the companies, or by accessing online information for updated financial reports.

A partial listing from the *Barron's* Earnings Scoreboard is shown in Figure 8.2.

This partial listing reveals the following information for the major surprises:

- *Headings.* The headings line shows that information reported includes company name, the period reported, the consensus estimate among industry analysts before actual reports were released, and the actual net earnings per share.
- *Positive and negative outcomes.* The two segments report positive results (actual was greater than estimates) and negative results (actual was lower than estimates). In the example, the first entry reveals that analysts believed Aurora Biosciences would report 5 cents per share for the second quarter. Actual results were 19 cents per share.

The scoreboard gives the following information for the week's major estimate changes:

- *Headings.* The headings line shows that information reported includes the company name, the fiscal year-end date for the companies being reported, the previous Friday's consensus, and the latest Friday's consensus.
- *Positive and negative outcomes.* These segments break out positive changes (increases in earnings estimates) and negative changes (decreases in earnings estimates). In the example, the first line reports that analysts changed their consensus about Internet.com, whose fiscal year ends in December. The previous Friday's consensus was that the company would earn 6 cents per share. The most recent consensus was that it would earn 11 cents per share.

Investor's Business Daily (IBD) provides earnings reports in the same basic format as the *Wall Street Journal.* However, *IBD* provides additional emphasis to highlight significant factors. Reports showing an upward change are listed first, and the number of "up" reports is given with the median change. This section is followed by the down listings, which also

---

FIGURE 8.3 Earnings News Summaries

Investor's Business Daily

Company & Symbol		Best Ups Last Qtr % Chg	Last Qtr Earnings	Last Qtr Sales	A-Tax Margin
Town & Country Trust	TCT	+620%	0.72 vs 0.10	+ 7%	+37.6%
ILOG SA ADR	ILOG	+550%	0.13 vs 0.02	+24%	+ 9.3%
Triton Energy Ltd. CL A	OIL	+436%	0.59 vs 0.11	+33%	+36.2%
		Most Downs			
Hercules Inc.	HPC	– 73%	0.15 vs 0.56	– 1%	+ 1.9%
Checkpoint SysInc.	CKP	– 57%	0.06 vs 0.14	+91%	+ 1.2%
M D C Corporation Inc A	MDCA	– 45%	0.16 vs 0.29	+27%	+ 1.2%

---

include the number of reports and the median change. The listings also include the current stock price, and the *IBD* rankings for relative price strength and earnings per share. A five-pointed star indicates that quarterly earnings are up 30 percent or more and that sales and earnings grew since the previous quarter. Sales and earnings are boldfaced in each listing, making these key features easy to locate. *IBD* augments its "Earnings News" section with a table summarizing the biggest gainers and losers. A partial listing table is shown in Figure 8.3.

This summary is helpful because it shows the biggest changes by company. However, the information can be somewhat confusing in the way it is presented. For example, one of the "most down" stocks shows a 91 percent upward gain in the last quarter's sales. Because earnings and sales are mixed on the same table, the information appears inconsistent. The rankings are based on earnings; the inclusion of sales figures causes confusion about what exactly is being reported. This type of scorekeeping is interesting, but it is only a moment's view of the market. For long-term investors, this information is of little or no lasting interest.

These tables show the company and symbol; the latest quarter's percentage change in earnings (the stocks are ranked by percentage change since the previous quarter); the latest quarter's earnings per share, shown for both the latest quarter and the previous quarter; the latest quarter's percentage change sales; and the percentage change in after-tax margin, also called after-tax profit. In the example, the first line reports that Town & Country Trust was the largest percentage gainer in earnings, which were up 620 percent from the prior quarter. The latest quarter's earnings were 72 cents per share, versus 10 cents per share in the previous quarter. Sales were up 7 percent since the previous year's quarter; and after-tax margin increased by 37.6 percent.

DIVIDENDS

Investors who consider themselves fundamentalists watch two primary indicators. The first is the earnings per share, and the second is the dividend declared and paid. Long-term investors judge corporations by their ability to declare dividends regularly, to maintain the yield; and to gradually increase payments to stockholders over time.

A corporation's board of directors declares a dividend per share and both a payable date and a record date. Payments to stockholders are the traditional way of disbursing dividends. However, an increasing trend is for investors to purchase additional partial shares rather than taking cash payments. Many listed companies set up procedures to enable shareholders to take part in such plans for reinvesting in partial shares. The plans are called DRIPs, or Dividend Reinvestment Plans.

The dividend is paid out (or issued in the form of additional shares) on the payable date, and they are paid to shareholders of record as of the record date. A company's dividend is said to "go ex-dividend" after the record date, meaning that to receive a dividend, an investor must own the stock on the ex-dividend date. The payable date always follows the record date, so divi-

---

FIGURE 8.4   Corporate Dividend News

The Wall Street Journal

Dividends reported August 7

Company	Period	Amt.	Payable Date	Record Date
		REGULAR		
Chesapeake Corp	Q	.22	11-15-00	10-13
Deluxe Corp	Q	.37	9-5-00	8-21
ECI Telecom	Q	.05	8-31-00	8-10
Eastern Co	Q	.11	9-15-00	8-25
		IRREGULAR		
Unisource Energy	Q	.08	9-8-00	8-15
	FUNDS—REITs—INVESTMENT COS—LPS			
CIM Hi Yld Secs	M	.0575	8-25-00	8-17
Carr America Realty	Q	.4625	9-1-00	8-18
Emerging Mkt Infra	—	.25	8-25-00	8-11

STOCK EX-DIVIDEND AUGUST 9

Company	Amount	Company	Amount
Bay State Bncp	.47	Bowne & Co	.055
Bay View Captl	.10	Bush Indus c1A	.05
Belo (AH) Corp	.07	Cabot Oil & Gas	.04
Boeing Co	.14	Church & Dwight	.07

---

dends will be paid out to investors who are shareholders as of the record date, even if they sell the stock after that date.

The *Wall Street Journal* provides a daily table summarizing all of the pertinent dividend news. A partial listing is shown in Figure 8.4

This partial listing shows the following:

- *Headings.* The dividends report for the day shows the company name, period reported (month or quarter), amount of dividend, payable date, and record date. In the example, the first line shows that the currently reported dividend for Chesapeake Corp. is a quarterly dividend of

---

FIGURE 8.5 Week's Dividend Payments

Barron's

NYSE

This list includes payouts on common shares and certain other securities, but not preferred stocks.

MONDAY		THURSDAY	
APT Satellite	.3594	Albertsons	.19
BritAir	2.0906	Bass	.1668
Masco	.12	CIGNA High	.06
TUESDAY		CtrptProp	.5025
BOC Gp	.6456	FRIDAY	
Suburbn Prpn	.525	ConsidPaper	.22
WEDNESDAY		GenlClb	.05
FleetwdEnt	.19	WestGasRes	.05

---

22 cents per share. It is to be paid out on November 15 to investors who were shareholders of record as of October 13.

- *Type of dividend.* Several types of dividends are reported: regular and irregular dividends and dividends of nonstock companies, including mutual funds, real estate investment trusts (REITs), mutual funds, and limited partnerships. Listings may also include categories for foreign company dividends, increased dividends, decreased dividends, initial dividends, and liquidations.

- *Ex-dividend.* This is an alphabetical listing of all companies going ex-dividend on the reported date. Shareholders of record on this date receive the most recently declared dividend on the payable date.

Investor's Business Daily reports this information in the same format, with one exception. In *IBD* the record date is shown before the payment date.

The *Barron's* summary of dividends is reported by exchange in the "Market Laboratory" section. In addition to dividends

FIGURE 8.6   Stock Splits/Dividends

Barron's

Company Name and Ticker Symbol	Amount	Payment Date	Record Date
Career Educ Inc.—CECO (NASDAQ)	2-for-1	8-25	8-14
Independence Hold—INHO (NASDAQ)	Stk. 10%	8-28	8-14
Merix Corp—MERX (NASDAQ)	3-for-2	8-25	8-10

payment summaries, *Barron's* provides two additional tables, one for stock splits and dividends, and the other for dividend payment boosts. A typical listing of the week's dividend payments is shown in Figure 8.5.

This is a day-by-day listing of dividends paid, given in summary form with company name and dividend per share.

Figure 8.6 shows the summary of stock splits and dividends in the *Barron's* "Market Laboratory" section. Splits normally involve the replacement of each share with two or more shares of lesser value. However, some splits involve payment or credit of additional dividends.

This partial listing shows:

- *Headings.* The company name, ticker symbol and exchange are provided in the first column, the amount and format of the split are given next, and the payment date and record date follow.
- *Specific listings.* The details of stock splits or dividends are provided on each line. The first line details a typical 2-for-1 split. Shareholders of record on August 14 will receive two shares for every share owned, and the change will take place on August 25. In the second line, we see that shareholders will receive 10 percent additional stock. For every 100 shares owned on the record date of August 14, shareholders will be given an additional 10 shares in place of a cash dividend. The shares will be transferred to stockholders on August 28.

FIGURE 8.7   Dividend Payment Boosts

Barron's

Company Name and Ticker Symbol	Period	To	From	Payment Date	Record Date
Amli Resident Prop—AML (NYSE)	Q	.47	.46	8-23	8-11
Briggs & Stratton—BGG (NYSE)	Q	.31	.30	10-2	8-24
Carlisle Cos—CSL (NYSE)	Q	.20	.18	9-1	8-17

Barron's also summarizes dividend boost reports, as shown in Figure 8.7.

This table reports the following information:

- *Headings.* This table reports the company name, ticker symbol, and exchange; the period (usually "Q" for quarterly dividend); the new dividend amount (to) and the old dividend (from); and payment and record dates.
- *Specific information.* The first line reports that the company's quarterly dividend was increased from 46 cents per share to 47 cents per share. Shareholders of record as of August 11 will receive the increased dividend, which will be paid out on August 23.

INSIDER TRANSACTIONS

Reports of insider transactions are another revealing form of fundamental information. Insiders are officers, directors, and owners of 10 percent or more of the company's stock. Insiders are required to report to the SEC in the month following any trade in the company's stock. Federal law requires that all information that affects the value of publicly traded stock be made available to the public. An insider is in the position to have more insight about a company's value, just by virtue of being an insider. Although this does not mean that an insider's transaction is based on information not available to the public, it does mean that the insider's knowledge of the company might be a significant factor to consider. In other words, if

FIGURE 8.8   Insider Transactions

Barron's

RECENT FILINGS
(In Latest Week)

PURCHASES

Company	Symbol (Exch)	% Chg. in Holdings	# of Insiders	# of Shares	$ Value
Johnson Controls	JCI (N)	333	1	5,000	272,500
Weyerhaeuser	WY (N)	150	1	300	14,025
Lillian Vernon	LVC (A)	100	1	2,000	22,000

SALES

Company	Symbol (Exch)	% Chg. in Holdings	# of Insiders	# of Shares	$ Value
Alberto Culver	ACV.A (N)	−100	1	993	22,839
Ben & Jerry's	BCIJA (O)	−100	1	3,845	167,642
Can-Cal Resources	CCRE (O)	−100	1	2,000	6,160

LARGEST % CHANGES IN INSIDER HOLDINGS
(Over Six Months)
INCREASES

Company	Symbol (Exch)	% Chg. in Holdings	# Insiders Buying	# Insiders Selling	# Shares Bought	# Shares Sold
Imagex.com	IMGX (O)	273	2	0	105,000	0
Johnson Controls	JCI (N)	272	2	0	5,400	0
PerkinElmer	PKI (N)	71	2	1	9,000	800

LARGEST % CHANGES IN INSIDER HOLDINGS
(Over Six Months)
DECREASES

Company	Symbol (Exch)	% Chg. in Holdings	# Insiders Buying	# Insiders Selling	# Shares Bought	# Shares Sold
Shaw Group	SGR (N)	− 42	0	6	0	108,402
Corsair Common	CAIR (O)	− 41	0	4	0	49,285
Alberto Culver	ACV.A (N)	− 38	0	2	0	4,993

insiders decide to buy, it could be a sign that it is time for others to buy as well.

Of the three major financial papers, only *Barron's* provides an analysis of insider transactions. The table is divided into four parts, and a sample is provided in Figure 8.8.

This table reports the following about recent purchases and sales:

1. and 2. *Company identification.* Recent filings are reported by company, ticker symbol, and exchange (A = Amex, N = NYSE, and O = Nasdaq). In the example, the first line under purchases reveals that Johnson Controls trades on the NYSE. The first line under sales shows that Alberto Culver also trades on the NYSE.
3. *Percentage change in holdings.* This is the percentage of increase or decrease in holdings among insiders. In the case of Johnson Controls, insider holdings increased 333 percent. One insider's holdings in Alberto Culver decreased 100 percent.
4. *Number of insiders.* This is the number of individual insiders trading stock for the week reported. In each of the samples listed under both purchases and sales, only one insider traded stock.
5. *Number of shares.* This column reports the number of shares bought. The one insider bought 5,000 shares in Johnson Controls, and the single insider sold 993 shares in Alberto Culver.
6. *Dollar value.* The Johnson Controls insider paid $272,500 for the 5,000 shares purchased, and the Alberto Culver insider sold the 993 shares for $22,839.

The table also reports the following about the largest percent changes in insider holdings over six months:

1. and 2. *Company identification.* The first two columns report company, symbol, and exchange. The first line under increases shows that Imagex.com trades with the

symbol IMGX on the Nasdaq. The Shaw Group trades with the symbol SGR on the NYSE.

3. *Percentage change in holdings.* This column shows the percentage of increase or decrease in holdings by corporate insiders. Imagex.com insider holdings increased by 273 percent. Shaw Group insider holdings decreased by 42 percent.

4. and 5. *Number of insiders buying or selling.* These two columns show the number of individuals who traded corporate stock in the previous six months. Two insiders bought Image.com stock and none sold it. Six insiders sold Shaw Group stock but none bought it.

6. and 7. *Number of shares bought and sold.* These columns show the number of corporate shares traded by insiders. Insiders bought 105,000 shares of Imagex.com stock, and insiders sold 108,402 shares of Shaw Group stock.

KEY POINT: Trends in insider transactions provide valuable information, but the causes for the specific trades vary considerably, so decisions to buy or sell should include information beyond insider transactions, which are just one piece of the bigger puzzle.

CORPORATE REPORTS

Every listed company is required to issue quarterly and annual reports, which are available to the public. Two major reports are filed with the SEC: Form 10-Q (the quarterly report) and Form 10-K (the annual report). These disclosure reports include current financial statements and extensive descriptions of corporate business and of the insiders—officers and major stockholders.

The contents of quarterly and annual reports are interesting for shareholders and for anyone thinking about buying stock

KEY POINT: The Securities and Exchange Commission (SEC) provides dozens of free documents for investors who are concerned with corporate disclosure and reporting. To order or download online, check the SEC Web site at *<www.sec.gov>*.

in a company. It helps to read reports in detail to become familiar with a company's products or services.

KEY POINT: Corporate earnings reports in the press usually include only the financial highlights. To see the full text of quarterly or annual reports for listed companies, go to the Web site *<http://biz.yahoo.com/reports/edgar.html>*, where you can download or read all of the reports filed in the most recent week.

In addition to the required disclosure documents filed with the SEC, companies issue annual reports of their own. These tend to be glossy, nicely designed public relations tools that include audited financial statements, messages from the president and CEO, colorful charts showing financial results and growth, photos and art about the company's products and services, and more. While these reports are useful and interesting, they are intended more as public relations documents than as disclosure documents.

KEY POINT: Annual reports can be ordered from any listed company. The easiest way to get annual reports instantly is to view them online. Dozens of sites, including *<reportgallery.com>*, *<www.annualreportservice.com>*, and *<www.prars.com>*, provide free access to corporate Web sites where reports can be reviewed.

There is no shortage of fundamental information, both on the Internet and from corporations and subscription services.

Two major suppliers of information on listed companies are Value Line Investment Survey and Standard & Poor's. Both of these organizations provide excellent subscription-based services with well-detailed analysis of both technical and fundamental information.

Brokerage houses also provide research reports for listed companies, and their analysis, which often is in-depth and interesting to shareholders, provides more critical points of view than you will ever find in the self-serving and less objective annual reports issued by companies themselves. However, a brokerage company's report might also be self-serving if the firm is operating as a dealer or is employed as an underwriter in the stock. Before accepting a brokerage firm's opinion on a company, ask what the firm's role is. The report will be objective only if the brokerage firm does not have a financial interest in making recommendations. Subscription services and brokerage reports are most valuable when they include soundly based forecasts of future fundamentals and investment opportunity or risk.

PUTTING FINANCIAL INFORMATION TO WORK

With such widespread availability of fundamental information, there is no reason that investors should operate without knowing all about the companies in their portfolio. In practice, however, the majority of investors follow only technical signals: day-to-day changes in stock prices, price volatility, and market indexes like the DJIA, for example. They pay little attention to fundamental information except when published reports are surprising in light of what analysts have predicted, and then invariably the market overreacts. If profits are lower than expected, the stock's price falls; if the report is better than expected, the price rises. These reactions normally correct themselves within a few days, but the irony of the market is that even though the fundamentals are recognized widely as being important, they are ignored for the most part. The majority of investors make their decisions based on short-term information, opinion, and price-related statistics.

> **KEY POINT:** It is ironic that even though so much importance is placed on the fundamentals, many investors make decisions impulsively or on the basis of nonfundamental information. That's because "easy" and "available" information is simple, but fundamental analysis has many variables and requires deeper understanding.

There is a significant problem associated with the way that fundamental information is reported in the market. The mentality of the stock market is to keep score. A company is judged as successful only if it outperforms its previous annual results, even if increases would not be practical or even desirable. Some industries can be expected to produce a predetermined level of net profits. So if, for example, companies in one of those industries can reasonably expect profits in the range of 6 to 8 percent, it makes no sense to judge a company if it fails to earn a 9 percent profit.

A company may have had profits last year of 6.5 percent, and the analysts may have estimated that this year's results will be 7.5 percent. However, actual results come in at 7 percent, the company's stock price falls. The news is "disappointing" because actual results are lower than those predicted by Wall Street experts. This can occur even if the company itself considers a 7 percent net profit as excellent, given its own forecasting and the nature of the industry.

The financial realities of corporate accounting are entirely separate from market analysis of sales and profits. The market demands that companies grow consistently and that stock prices reward growth with value growth in dollar share. The market will punish lack of growth with a falling stock price.

However, none of these cause-and-effect market realities are in conformity with accounting or fundamental realities, for a number of reasons.

> **KEY POINT:** You should make a clear distinction between financial reporting as it takes place in accounting departments, and fundamental analysis as it takes place in the market. There are very few points of agreement between the two.

Growth and expansion are not always desirable. The market does not take into consideration the fact that one of management's jobs is to plan and control growth. It is not always a good outcome to exceed the previous year's sales or profits, especially when expansion occurs at the expense of customer service. Many leaders of well-managed corporations recognize that it makes more sense to achieve a manageable level of activity and to resist growth beyond that level. The myth that companies that don't grow are doomed to fail is just that, a myth. However, the stock market is blind to the fundamental considerations and wants only to see growth in sales and profits each and every year.

> **KEY POINT:** Sometimes the responsible thing for a company to do is to curtail growth if it is taking place too quickly. The corporate manager who cuts back risks being punished by the market by way of falling stock prices, but the astute long-term investor appreciates the value of responsible management decisions.

Markets are limited and finite. It simply makes no sense to believe that a company can continue to expand indefinitely. Any product or service will find only a limited market. There is no such thing as unlimited growth, because market demand can go only so far. Still, it is a "market sin" to say this is so.

> **KEY POINT:** The finite nature of business markets is at odds with the market philosophy that there are no limits to potential growth. The lack of connection between market expectations and business realities accounts for a lot of the inaccuracy in so-called market expertise and prediction.

Competitive forces tend to limit growth for an entire sector. Free markets are efficient in many respects, tending to reward well-managed companies with growth while smaller, poorly capitalized companies tend to go out of business. However, each company in a sector has to share expansion with the sector's strongest members. No entity owns an entire market, and well-conceived products and services tend to have strong competitors. This limits how much growth any one company can achieve over one year, five years, or more.

> **KEY POINT:** Competition is the real driving force in the business world, but the market is preoccupied with stock prices—the ups and downs of daily change—and is not likely to acknowledge the real limitations on growth that come with competition.

These are only some of the factors affecting the potential expansion of a listed company. Because the market requires that a company always exceed its previous year's results, unrealistic demands are placed on the fundamental reporting of listed companies. Prices reflect the market's approval or disapproval, if only for the short term.

The specific forms of reporting by the financial press are limited in value, because the press emphasizes technical rather than fundamental indicators. To a degree, when the press attempts to report fundamental information, it does so in a way that is similar to the way it reports technical indicators. Great emphasis is placed on the biggest percentage gainers in earnings, the week's biggest surprises, the greatest differences between estimates and actual outcomes. For the serious student of fundamental reporting, comparisons such as these are of limited value and interest. Of greater interest are the specific internal comparisons of corporate results.

> **KEY POINT:** The only worthwhile fundamental comparison is made between reporting periods. The market, however, likes to compare companies to one another, even when their products or services are completely unrelated. This in inane, but popular.

Earnings reports are helpful summaries because the information can be digested quickly. They include year-to-year comparisons for the same quarter and enable the financial reader to see whether fundamental results are up or down from the previous period. It would be helpful if financial reporting placed a greater emphasis on the *reasons* for changes from one year to the next. Every corporate report includes explanations for changes between the periods being compared. It might not be practical to include all of those explanations with the brief reports in the press, but some major highlights would be helpful. A reader who is interested in a specific company needs to do research. The reports in the financial press are valuable, but only as starting points for more in-depth study. The Internet is a valuable research tool for this purpose.

The earnings scoreboard approach to reporting fundamental information reflects the market's mentality about all forms of reporting. Who did better than the year before, and who did worse? More specifically, which companies were the biggest winners, and which were the biggest losers? The financial press likes to highlight information that can be compiled from a database of fundamental results, but the same press provides

> **KEY POINT:** Use the Internet to find annual or quarterly reports. For more information, use the same sources to find corporate headquarters' Web sites. Write to the investor relations departments of companies whose stock you are thinking of purchasing if you need more in-depth information about the stock.

very little in the way of thoughtful analysis. Analysis is not the job of the press; it is up to each investor to interpret the raw data.

The newspapers' "best and worst" approach may be appropriate for the study of stock prices and volatility and for sector analysis. However, when it comes to the fundamental results for individual companies, the newspapers are of little value. Serious investors will find it is best to perform real research on target companies with the use of online resources or through investor relations departments of companies. Because thousands of corporations are listed in the newspapers, the majority of reported information is of little or no interest or relevance to most people. Serious fundamental analysis might begin when an investor flags an item in a newspaper table, but the real work requires going beyond the press reports and getting more detailed company-specific information. To judge a company's fundamental strength and growth potential, you need to become a competent analyst in your own right. You need to review the SEC filings for the company, the audited financial statements and annual reports published by the company, and the position of the company in its sector and compared to its major competitors.

> **KEY POINT:** The fundamental comparisons that appear in the press are of no value to the serious analyst. But the internal year-to-year comparisons of one company's sales and earnings are significant, whether or not they make it onto one of the financial newspapers' lists.

Dividend reporting in the paper media has many of the same flaws as price and earnings reporting. The reports are generalized and tend to show only what occurred in the past week without any in-depth explanations for specific companies. In practical terms, it is impossible for the newspapers to analyze dividend trends in any depth. Again, although the format of dividend reports cannot help investors make decisions about their specific holdings, investors can use the raw data to perform more research. It is not the dividend being paid next quarter, but the trend and history of dividend payments that reveals what is going on in a listed company. In other words, you should determine whether the company has paid dividends regularly, without missing any quarters; whether the dividend has been consistent, whether it has grown as the corporation's market position has grown; and whether you can use dividend information to predict growth in the future. A serious study of dividend trends provides important fundamental information, and the preliminary data presented in the press may signal significant changes worth investigating further.

> **KEY POINT:** It is the *trend* in dividend payments—in consistency as well as growth—that defines a company's ability to provide shareholders with consistent returns. For this, you need ongoing analysis over many years.

One of the more useful forms of fundamental information is the table provided each week by *Barron's* summarizing insider transactions. An insider is a knowledgeable investor whose decision to buy or sell *might* be useful information to you. But again, further research is required, because you cannot know from the table why the transactions occurred. For example, a particular executive might sell stock upon retirement; that does not constitute an alarm for other investors. The table shows the number of insiders making trades. When that number is high, it could represent an important trend, or it could be meaningless. Only with additional research will you be able to discover whether insider transactions are important to your decision of whether to buy, hold, or sell shares.

TELEVISION AND RADIO FINANCIAL REPORTING

A wide variety of television and radio programs present investment news and information on several levels. With the limited available time and the necessity of keeping viewer interest, both general television news and the specialized investment-oriented variation tend to be shallow in content. These shows tend to be dominated by the high points, like major moves in the Dow Jones Industrial Average, reports of the biggest gainers and losers, and headline news about specific companies. No in-depth analysis is provided.

Radio shows, on the other hand, tend to be oriented toward answering caller questions providing popular information such as answers to frequently asked questions on the part of a listening audience. Both television and radio have one problem in common: viewers and listeners have no control over what information is provided. They cannot pick and choose as they can with newspapers and on the Internet. As a television viewer or radio listener, you are in a passive position; you see or hear whatever the show provides, no more and no less.

Some programs, even with the limited-time problem, do provide very useful information. Television programs, which are more likely than radio programs to be directed to a national audience, sometimes cover topics in considerable detail and often include guest interviewees with a particular point of view or specialized information to share.

Here are five guidelines for selecting worthwhile television financial programs:

1. Look for shows that provide you with information, such as interviews with experts in the field, that goes beyond the news that is available in other media.

2. Make a distinction between popular reporting and in-depth coverage. Most shows offer a mix of both, and being aware of the difference helps you to select information that will stimulate insights and further your research.

3. For updated daily coverage, select programs that cover national trends and news, rather than shows that are strictly local. The market is national and international, and while news of local stocks is interesting, it does not provide you with the global view that you need in today's market.

4. Avoid watching television shows that are transparent and only offer heated-over stories from other sources. Not only are these stories of no value to you in managing your portfolio; they also tend to be out of date by the time you see them.

5. Look for serious televised programming of financial news, and watch regularly, whether daily or weekly. Check out the *Bloomberg Small Business Show* (USA), *Bulls and Bears* (Fox News), *Cavuto Business Report* (Fox News), *Moneyweek* (CNN), *Your Money* (CNN), *Cavuto on Business* (Fox News), *Wall Street Journal Report* (NBC), *CBS MarketWatch Weekend* (CBS), and *Wall Street Week* (PBS).

When selecting radio shows, keep the following three guidelines in mind:

1. Watch for a bias on the part of the host, and recognize that one person's point of view does not always apply to everyone.

2. Seek out shows that include in-depth interviews with experts, especially programs that are live and allow callers to call in and ask questions. These types of shows often provide some of the best information sources.

3. Recognize that while short radio programs can be informative, time limitations make it very difficult to go into

a lot of analysis. Shorter-duration radio programs tend to gloss over the information that you need the most.

If your interests are short term and you want to get in and out of market positions rapidly, the financial press is well suited for you. However, if you see yourself as a long-term investor, it is a mistake to rely on the financial press for any information of long-term value. It's important to keep informed of market trends, corporate news, and the various fundamental and technical indicators; however, you also need to make distinctions between today's news and the equally important long-term interpretation of that news in ways that guide you clearly along the way.

It is important to recognize that the financial media are more comfortable reporting technical information than the fundamentals. They place great emphasis on the averages of the overall market and on keeping the score of market prices. It makes little sense to report fundamental and technical information in the same way, but the newspapers do it anyway. The information provided by the financial press has value as a starting point only. You can use the raw data of fundamental reporting to do further research and to get more in-depth answers for yourself. It is a mistake to assume that the financial reports in the newspapers provide in-depth or reliable information. The financial news is just a starting point.

CHAPTER 9

Economic Indicators

Business more than any other occupation is a continual dealing with the future; it is a continual calculation, an instinctive exercise in foresight.

–Henry R. Luce *(Fortune,* October 1960)

The two primary schools of thought about market analysis are the fundamental and the technical, as most investors know. A third, less popular school of thought about securities analysis is based on broader economics. Analysts disagree about whether the study of economic indicators is valid for the purpose of helping the investor to manage a personal portfolio of investments.

Arguments in favor of economic analysis include the point that the economic health of the country affects the stock and bond markets. So studying trends in the economy is a sound method to apply when timing and making market decisions. However, a problem with this argument is that individual stocks do not always behave in conformity with larger measurements. This is a problem with any form of broad analysis, including analysis of market averages like the DJIA as well as analysis of the overall economy. Each stock tends to behave in a manner that is based on the economics of the individual company, and not based so much on what is happening with the economy at large. Of course, sectors like recreation may tend to suffer in terms of sales and profits when the economy is poor, because people will spend less on nonnecessities; and utility stocks may perform better when interest rates are low, because they depend on debt capitalization to a greater degree than other industrial companies. Overall sector performance tends to affect the sector's individual members even when the companies' numbers do not justify changes in their stock's price.

It is questionable whether economic indicators are valid forms of information for managing a small individual portfolio. It does not hurt to review information from time to time about the relative health of the economy, but most analysts recognize that broad economics are removed from the more relevant fundamental and technical indicators unique to each company.

KEY POINT: The effects of the overall economy on a specific stock's investment value often are unclear or too far removed to be used exclusively as a means for making investment decisions. Economic indicators are useful only in a broad, comparative sense.

Many investors who are oriented toward math and statistics take comfort in numbers and include economic analysis in their program. However, it also makes sense to recognize that economic analysis should be an adjunct to a larger program of analysis, and certainly should not be a primary source for information upon which decisions will be based.

ECONOMIC INDICATORS

Three overall indexes are used to measure the U.S. economy: the Index of Leading Economic Indicators, the Coincident Index, and the Lagging Index. These indexes are watched not only in the United States, but worldwide as well. The U.S. economy has direct influence on the major economies of Europe and Asia, especially in the financial arena. These statistical indicators are believed to have predictive value for the U.S. economy, although the timing of cyclical change is always rather elusive. The Index of Leading Economic Indicators is believed to signal changes in the aggregate economy in advance; changes in the Coincident Index are believed to occur at the same time as cyclical economic change; and changes in the Lagging Index are believed to follow overall cyclical change.

The Index of Leading Economic Indicators

The Index of Leading Economic Indicators is a combination of ten measurements of economic activity, weighted with a standardization factor so that some indicators have greater weight than others. Money supply and interest rates account for more than half of the weighting, and other indicators, such as new orders by manufacturers of nondefense goods, are given less influence. The following indicators are shown in order of their weighting, or standardization factor, from largest to smallest:

1. *Interest rate spread, 10-year Treasury bonds less federal funds.* The interest rate spread is the difference between long-term and short-term rates and is also called the yield curve. It measures sentiment concerning monetary policy. When the curve is negative (because short-term rates are higher than long-term rates) it is seen as an indicator of coming recession. *Standardization factor: .332*
2. *Money supply.* This is a measurement of money in circulation—currency, demand deposits, checkable deposits, travelers checks, savings deposits, small denomination

time deposits, and balances in money market mutual funds. *Standardization factor: .301*

3. *Average weekly hours, manufacturing.* This is a measurement of the average hours worked per week by production employees. This is included in the index in the belief that the manufacturing sector is a leader in economic trends and that companies tend to make adjustments in their labor hours before making major changes in their workforce. *Standardization factor: .184*

4. *Manufacturers' new orders, consumer goods and materials.* This is the level of purchases by consumers as reflected in manufacturers' statistics. *Standardization factor: .050*

5. *Stock prices, 500 common stocks.* This is the S&P 500 stock index, which is recognized as a broad measurement of market prices in the New York Stock Exchange. *Standardization factor: .031*

6. *Vendor performance, slower deliveries diffusion index.* This measures the time it takes for industrial companies to receive goods ordered from suppliers. The index increases as delivery time slows down, because the slowdown is believed to be a reflection of increased demand for manufacturing supplies. *Standardization factor: .028*

7. *Average weekly claims for unemployment insurance.* This counts new claims filed for unemployment. As the numbers increase, the news is worse for the economy; thus, the statistic is inverted. *Standardization factor: .025*

8. *Building permits, new private housing units.* The number of building permits issued is a measurement of construction volume and is believed to be a dependable measurement of housing, one component of economic production. *Standardization factor: .019*

9. *Index of consumer expectations.* This is intended to measure the mood of consumers about future economic conditions. Individuals are surveyed about whether they

believe the following are positive, negative, or un-changed: their family's economic prospects for the coming year; the nation's economic prospects for the coming year; and the nation's economic prospects for the coming five years. *Standardization factor: .018*

10. *Manufacturers' new orders, nondefense capital goods.* This measures quantity of new orders received in capital-goods-sector industries. *Standardization factor: .013*

The Coincident Index

The Coincident Index has four components that are weighted as follows:

1. *Employees on nonagricultural payrolls.* Also broadly called payroll employment, this is a statistical count of full-time and part-time workers (no distinction is made between permanent and temporary workers). *Standardization factor: .479*

2. *Personal income less transfer payments.* This is income from all sources, excluding transfer payments such as Social Security. It is the amount most wage earners think of as available income. *Standardization factor: .283*

3. *Index of industrial production.* This is a measurement of production output in specific sectors: manufacturing, mining, and gas and electric utility companies. *Standardization factor: .129*

4. *Manufacturing and trade sales.* This measures sales at several levels: in manufacturing, wholesale, and retail. *Standardization factor: .109*

The Lagging Index

The Lagging Index has seven components also weighted:

1. *Average prime rate charged by banks.* This is an average of bank rates, changes in which tend to lag behind general economic activity. *Standardization factor: .243*
2. *Ratio, consumer installment credit outstanding to personal income.* This measures individual debt of consumers in comparison to income. *Standardization factor: .221*
3. *Change in Consumer Price Index for services.* This is a change in the service component of the Consumer Price Index. *Standardization factor: .186*
4. *Commercial and industrial loans outstanding.* This is the level of loan balances held by banks and nonfinancial companies. *Standardization factor: .128*
5. *Ratio of manufacturing and trade inventories to sales.* This is a measurement of the rate of inventory to sales for a broad range of companies. *Standardization factor: .123*
6. *Changes in labor cost per unit of output, manufacturing.* This is a measure of change in the cost of labor for manufacturing firms, expressed on a per-unit-of-production basis. *Standardization factor: .062*
7. *Average duration of unemployment.* This counts the number of weeks that people are unemployed. It is inverted in the index because increases in the duration of unemployment have a negative impact on the economy. *Standardization factor: .037*

None of the three major financial papers publish regular summaries of the these indexes, even though they are the standards by which economic activity is measured and predicted. Of the three papers, only *Barron's* publishes an extensive summary of economic indicators, in its "Market Laboratory" section of the paper. It would make little sense for the papers to summarize the economic indexes daily, because these statistics are neither released nor updated daily.

WEEKLY ECONOMICS TABLES IN *BARRON'S*

Barron's includes two full pages of economic indicators, including the three indexes, each week. The nicely detailed listings provide a good overview of interest rates, money supply, metals prices, economic measurements, and real estate.

Interest Rates

A money fund report with money rates for major instruments provides a weekly overview of current interest and a comparison with recent rates. Figure 9.1 shows a typical *Barron's* Money Fund Report.

This table provides a nice overview of interest rates being paid on money market (short-term) instruments, including taxable and tax-exempt funds. (A tax-exempt fund will yield less interest because the rates compete net of taxes, whereas taxable fund income is subject to tax.) The columns provide useful comparisons between the current week, the previous week, and a year ago. The table lists sources for the information, including address and telephone number.

A highly detailed breakdown of interest rates for many financial instruments is also shown in the *Barron's* weekly summary. It is beyond the scope of this book to duplicate this table in detail; those interested in money markets and interest rates will find the *Barron's* summary a helpful source of information.

Money Supply

The money supply can be measured in several different ways. *Barron's* reports on Federal Reserve data and money supply as measured by M1, M2, and M3. (M1 is all coin and currency in circulation, travelers checks, checking account balances, NOW accounts, and credit union balances. M2 includes M1 plus savings and small time deposits, overnight repurchase

---

FIGURE 9.1   Money Fund Report

Barron's

Taxable Funds Aug. 1	Last Week	Prev. Week	Year Ago
Asset Levels (Bil. $)	1,450.7	1,446.7	1,245.56
Maturity, days	50	51	57
7-day comp. yld. %	6.16	6.14	4.60
7-day simple yld. %	5.98	5.96	4.50
30-day comp. yld. %	6.13	6.13	4.56
30-day simple yld. %	5.96	5.95	4.46

Taxable Funds July 31	Last Week	Prev. Week	Year Ago
Asset Levels (Bil. $)	215.4	215.6	192.19
Maturity, days	41	42	47
7-day comp. yld. %	3.68	3.60	2.61

Source: MoneyNet, Inc., a subsidiary of Informa Financial Information, Inc., One Research Drive, Westborough, MA 01581 (508) 616-6600.

Money Market Funds # (Bil. $)	Last Week	Prev. Week	Year Ago
Total Assets Aug. 2	1,716.0	1,701.0	1,480.0

Source: Investment Company Institute, 1401 H Street NW, Suite 1200, Washington, D.C. 20005-2148 (202) 326-5800.

---

agreements, and noninstitutional money market accounts. M3 is M2 plus large time deposits, repurchase agreements having maturity of longer than one day, and institutional money market accounts.)

The *Barron's* Federal Reserve Data Bank appears in Figure 9.2.

This table provides statistical and comparative data for the banks comprising the Federal Reserve System. The reported information relates to all of the member banks collectively and is of significant interest to those who follow the banking industry and are interested in using Fed information to track overall trends.

FIGURE 9.2   Federal Reserve Data Bank

Barron's

Member Bank Reserve Chgs. (Mil. $)	Latest Week	Prev. Week Change	Year Ago Change
U.S. Govt. securities:			
Bought outright	506,448	+155	+20,893
Held under repurch.	. . .	. . .	− 2,733
Federal agency secur:			
Bought outright	140	. . .	−109
Held under repurch.	. . .	. . .	− 3,630
Reserve bank credit:			
Adjustment credit	38	+26	−36
Seasonal borrowings	569	+20	+ 04
Extended credit	. . .	. . .	. . .
Float	1,340	+ 56	+581
Other F.R. assets	35,547	−38	+1,300
Total Fed. credit #	558,836	+535	+31,324
Gold stock	11,046	. . .	−1
SDR certif. accounts	4,200	. . .	−4,000
Treas. curr. outst.	29,797	+14	+2,646
Total acceptances	603,880	+550	+29,970
Currency in circ.	568,410	+14	+33,915
Treas. Cash Holdings	119	+17	+62
Treas. Fed Deposits	5,106	+473	+1
Foreign Fed Deposits	90	−2	−130
Other Fed deposits	235	+18	−15
Serv. related bal.	6,553	−284	−457
Other F.R. liab./cap.	15,449	−343	−2,823
Total factors	595,964	−124	+30,554
Reserves F.R. banks	7,916	+674	−584
Fgn. hold U.S. debt	703,658	+13	N.A.
Reserve Aggregates (Mil. $ sa)			
Total reserves	40,216	39,962	42,261
Nonborrowed reserves*	39,667	39,373	41,995
Required reserves**	39,198	38,722	41,312
Excess reserves	1,018	1,240	948
Borrowed reserves	549	589	266
Free reserves***	469	651	682
Monetary base	577,459	576,739	541,725

*Fed supply of permanent reserves provided.
**Demand for reserves to back deposits.
***Free reserves equal excess reserves minus discount window borrowings other than extended credit. Free reserves are a shorthand method of determining the degree of ease of Fed policy, or when they are negative net borrowed reserves, tightness.

FIGURE 9.3   Federal Reserve Key Assets and Liabilities

U.S. Banks (Bil. $)	Latest Week	Prev. Week Change
Bank credit	3,746.9	+ 0.5
Comm/industrial loans	1,077.1	+ 3.8
Loans to individuals	516.4	+ 0.6
Real estate loans	1,596.3	− 4.0
Home equity loans	115.9	+ 0.5
U.S. Govt. securities	813.8	− 2.1
Other securities	496.6	+ 9.0
Key Liabilities		
Transaction deposits	630.1	+21.1
Savings/other deposits	3,091.5	+ 5.7
Includes large deposits	916.0	+ 3.2

Barron's also reports on assets and liabilities of U.S. Banks, as shown in Figure 9.3.

This report is interesting because it reports on the mix of outstanding loans and credit, as well as week-to-week changes. Anyone following trends in interest rates and lending can use this information to watch trends in the banking industry and to forecast likely changes in the money supply and lending policies.

Metals Prices

The *Barron's* report on metals includes a mix of information, including statistics on metal mining and pricing. Some market watchers believe that the prices of precious metals react to or predict changes in stock market pricing and the overall health of the economy. Recent historical pricing patterns have made the metals market less useful as an economic predictor. *Barron's* report is summarized in Figure 9.4.

These metals price updates reflect weekly information and include comparisons with the previous year. *Barron's* also lists the sources for current information, which may vary from week to week.

FIGURE 9.4   Metals Statistics

Barron's

BARRON'S GOLDMINING INDEX

12-Month			8/03	7/27	Year Ago	Week % Chg.
High	**Low**					
433.68	253.54	Gold mining	253.54	257.14	336.35	– 1.40

GOLD & SILVER PRICES

	8/04	7/28	Year Ago
Gold, troy ounce	**8/04**	278.10	255.75
Silver, troy ounce	273.95	5.01	5.44

Base for pricing gold or silver contents of shipments and for making refining settlements.

Coins	Price	Premium $	Premium %
Krugerrand	275.20	2.00	.75
Maple Leaf	276.20	3.00	1.12
Mexican Peso	331.00	1.40	.51
Austria Crown	269.70	2.00	.73
Austria Phil	276.20	3.00	1.12
U.S. Eagles	276.20	3.00	1.12

Premium is the amount over the value of the gold content in the coin.

PLATINUM COIN PRICES

Coins	Coin Price Per Ounce	Premium $	Premium %
Canadian Maple Leaf	589.00	16.20	2.83
Isle of Man Noble	589.00	16.20	2.83
Amer. Eagle Bullion	589.00	16.20	2.83

Premium is the amount over the value of the platinum content in the coin.
Spot platinum price is $572.80.

The platinum coin prices report three things: coin price per ounce; dollar amount of the premium (value above spot platinum price for the day); and the percentage of premium. In the example, spot platinum price was $572.80 (coin price per ounce of $589.00 less premium of $16.20). The premium percentage is 2.83 percent ($16.20 divided by $572.80).

Economic Measurements

While *Barron's* does not specifically list current values of the three major economic indexes, it does include a half-page summary of key indicators called "Pulse of the Economy." This section covers many of the areas included in the three major economic indexes, but in a different arrangement. This hodge-podge of information may confuse people who are accustomed to studying indicators in other formats; however, for the market, arrangements of information in *Barron's* is suitable and easy to comprehend.

Figure 9.5 summarizes a typical report in the *Barron's* weekly "Pulse of the Economy" section.

In this sample listing, the factors noted with an *a* are based on a 1992 base of 100. Capacity utilization reflects the degree of capacity for the reported period. In the example, utilization occurred at 82.1 percent. Gross domestic product is reported as a percentage increase over the previous quarter. The last four lines report dollar values in billions. Thus, economic factors are reported in a variety of manners. Comparisons to the previous year are useful for tracking changes in the economic factors. The base of 100 is arbitrary, but it does enable economic analysts to make comparisons, both between different economic factors and between periods.

One problem with economic reporting is that it is not always accurate in terms of current spending patterns. For example, the consumer price index is based on buying patterns and trends of the 1980s and 1990s. It does not reflect the revolution in personal computing or the trend toward online commerce, but it is based on more traditional methods of purchasing consumer goods—going to a store, seeing a product, and buying it. Furthermore, the indexes are largely based on manufacturing and production and less on services. As the methods of reporting economic trends get more and more out of touch, the changes in various indexes become less reflective of the economic realities at play. Other major economic indicators

FIGURE 9.5   Economic Growth and Investment

	Latest Date	Latest Data	Preceding Period	Year Ago
Durable goods produced a	June	p189.7	r188.4	172.2
Capacity utilization %	June	p82.1	r82.2	80.5
Gross domestic product	2nd qtr	+ 5.2	r + 4.8	+ 2.5
Industrial outlet a	June	p144.6	r144.3	136.6
Manufacturing a	June	p150.5	r150.0	141.4
Nondurable goods produced a	June	p113.2	113.4	113.3
Personal income (Bil. $)	May	8,234	r8,203	7,792
All fixed investment	2nd qtr	1,793.6	r1,730.9	1,607.1
Non-residential investment	2nd qtr	1,426.2	r1,365.3	1,237.5
Residential investment	2nd qtr	375.0	r371.4	370.9

a—1992 equals 100   p—preliminary   r—revised

include statistics on production, consumption and distribution, inventories, orders, trade, inflation, employment, and construction.

A final segment in the *Barron's* "Pulse of the Economy" section summarizes the national debt and current deficits. A typical table for this section appears in Figure 9.6.

This summary reports on the federal debt as well as consumer buying and credit trends. It provides useful ongoing statistics for tracking public and private changes in these areas. To some extent, debt and spending trends may affect investments in the stock market, so these statistics are useful for investors who believe that economic indicators are useful.

Real Estate

A final section included in the weekly *Barron's* report concerns real estate performance as measured by several real estate sources. A typical listing is shown in Figure 9.7.

FIGURE 9.6   American Debt and Deficits

Barron's

	Latest Report	Preceding Report	Year Ago Report
Federal budget deficit (Bil. $) a	+124FY'99	+70FY'98	–23FY'97
Budget surplus/deficit (Bil. $) b	+56.28	–3.61	+53.57
Trade deficit (Bil. $, sa) c	–31.04	–30.50	– 21.34
Treasury gross public debt (Bil. $) d	5,652.5	5,670.7	5,613.2
Treasury statutory debt limit (Bil. $) d	5,950.0	5,950.0	5,950.0
Consumer installment debt (Bil. $) e	1,436.8	1,425.9	1,331.3
Mtg. Bankers Assoc. Refinance Index f	346.0	359.6	458.1
Mtg. Bankers Assoc. Purchase Index f	306.6	313.1	293.4

Sources: a-Office of Management and Budget. b-Monthly Treasury Statement.
c-Monthly Commerce Dept. Report. d-Daily Treasury Statement.
e-Monthly Federal Reserve Release. f-Weekly Seasonally Adjusted Mortgage.
Bankers Association of America Release (Base period: March 16, 1990 = 100.0)

These summaries show real estate activity and trends as measured by industry funds, pools, and management companies. Because the table is broken down both by type of real estate and by region, the information is especially useful for compiling real estate reports and for tracking returns on investments over time.

PUTTING ECONOMIC INDICATORS TO WORK

It would be quite easy for an investor to become buried in numbers and deluged with information to the point that decisions are impossible. The problem is not finding information, but discriminating between very useful, not very useful, and useless information.

When it comes to economic indicators, you face the twofold problem of not knowing how reliable the numbers are and not knowing how each statistic affects the market. An abundance of discussion about the relationship between economic indica-

FIGURE 9.7   Real Estate Performance Averages

	Barron's				
	Mar	Dec	Sep	Jun	Prev Mar
NCREIF Prop. Index (Mil. $)	82,820.8	77,432.3	75,676.6	72,780.8	68,056.8
Apts.	17.1%	16.9%	16.3%	16.4%	16.6%
Industrial	16.1	16.6	16.3	16.0	16.1
Office	42.0	41.9	42.6	42.2	40.7
Retail	23.5	24.3	23.5	24.1	25.4
East	28.5	28.7	28.5	28.6	28.8
Midwest	16.1	16.0	16.6	16.8	16.3
South	22.2	22.1	21.8	22.1	21.6
West	33.2	33.2	33.0	32.6	33.3
Total return	2.31	2.94	2.77	2.60	3.59
Wilshire RE Index (Mil. $)	113,460	113,090	115,463	130,676	116,974
Total return	2.81%	0.23%	(9.54)%	10.62%	(3.47)%
Dividend return	1.79	2.28	1.54	1.58	1.66
Wilshire REIT Index					
Total return	2.99	0.17	(8.27)	10.56	(4.10)
Dividend return	1.91	2.49	2.11	1.73	1.76
Wilshire REOC Index					
Total return	0.88	0.84	(19.95)	10.97	3.44
Dividend return	0.69	0.30	0.49	0.37	0.55

Sources: National Council of Real Estate Investment Fiduciaries, Two Prudential Plaza, 180 N. Stetson Avenue, Suite 2515, Chicago, IL 60601; Wilshire Asset Management, 1299 Ocean Avenue, Suite 700, Santa Monica, CA 90401-1085.

tors and the market remains inconclusive because it is impossible to *prove* how the economy interacts with the market.

Certain isolated economic indicators are extremely useful as some of many types of information that you can gather and use for making investment decisions. However, the more generalized your information is, the less useful it is for making decisions about any one particular stock.

Every economic statistic has value and meaning to someone, but not necessarily to everyone. You cannot conclude that an economic indicator is valuable unless you can establish a correlation between the report and the performance of your stock. This is the same problem faced by every investor who tries to time investment decisions on the basis of movement in the Dow Jones Industrial Average (DJIA). The DJIA tells you nothing about when to buy or sell a specific stock, and economic indicators have the same limitation.

> **KEY POINT:** By their nature, economic statistics are broad and are applicable to the overall economy, and the more broad your analysis, the less useful it is.

Some people want to believe that trends in mining, business inventories, new factory orders, the production of durable goods, or the balance of trade, will somehow be useful forecasting systems for predicting changes in market price or for identifying good or bad investments, or emerging sector leaders. Investors often want to identify an edge that gives them better-than-average information. The truth is, economic indicators and other statistical measurements are too broad to be of any use. They include data collected from the entire market, so using this information for any specific investment decision is ill-advised. Economic indicators are interesting for overall assessment of mood and economic trends, but they cannot help you to determine whether the timing is right to sell shares of a particular stock. For that, you need to study the economics of the individual corporation, also known as the fundamentals.

> **KEY POINT:** The only useful economic information for individual decisions is a study of the company's own economics, or financial information. It all comes back to the fundamentals.

Economic indicators are collected and reported in the methods described in this chapter for several reasons, not all of which lead to the indicators' usefulness to investors. These reasons include:

1. *Difficulty in getting current, reliable information.* Imagine collecting information from every company and individual in the country. It is quite a daunting task, and it requires considerable time and effort. Statistics about the economy generally are useful only if they also are current; thus, we see a lot of preliminary and revised totals—because it simply is impossible to get current, reliable information every week. Economic statistics are constantly adjusted.

2. *Complexity in the methods of gathering, summarizing, and reporting information.* The methods employed to summarize and report economic information are not simple. They involve collecting data from many different sources and then adjusting it. Much of the reporting involves making changes in index levels on the basis of an arbitrary base of 100 established several years in the past. Other statistics are seasonally adjusted (the notation *sa* in the newspaper tables identifies these), so they are by nature only estimates, and therefore inherently unreliable.

3. *Tradition in methods of reporting.* Some economic statistics are developed and tracked and become the norm for future reports, continuing to be used even when they are no longer valid. As the economy becomes globalized, balance of trade between countries is a less meaningful indicator than it might have been many years ago. Great importance is placed on industrial and manufacturing statistics related to production, orders, and inventories; however, as large segments of the world economy have turned increasingly to Internet technology and information services, the traditional method of reporting has not changed, so how reliable is the information? We cannot know. It has been said that "if all economists were laid end to end, they would not reach a conclusion."* This is

---

*Attributed to George Bernard Shaw.

a commentary on the nature of statistical information—it is complex and difficult to understand and interpret.

Some specific problems associated with economic statistics make the entire study of them questionable in terms of their use for investment management. If you own a small but diversified portfolio of stocks, directly or through mutual funds, you have to ask how broad economic indicators affect your holdings. Because no one really knows the answer, and because a company's performance is going to be the result of the company's individual circumstances, economic indicators are suspect at best.

For example, the balance of payments, also called the trade deficit or surplus, measures the difference between imports and exports. If the United States imports more than it exports, then it is said to have a negative balance of trade. Consumption that exceeds production, in other words, is believed to be a negative for the economy. However, this conclusion does not necessarily affect the long-term value of stock that you own. In fact, it might have nothing to do with your corporate stock holdings at all, especially if you own shares in companies with international operations. In addition, the trade deficit compares the United States with countries like China, whose population is significantly higher, and with Japan, whose population is significantly lower. The overall balance of trade does not reflect the true market for merchandise, because the number of consumers varies among countries.

For another example, one major area of reporting involves employment statistics. Economists study the civil labor force, nonfarm and government payrolls, a help-wanted index, and the unemployment rate. However, these statistics do not include the significant and growing number of self-employed individuals and owners of small companies. The unemployment rate is based on the available data: numbers of applications for unemployment and of people receiving payments. Not counted are people whose benefits have run out and others who are unemployed but not qualified for unemployment–potentially large numbers of people.

Barron's is the only financial paper to provide a comprehensive weekly summary of economic indicators. However, the format of the summary is mixed up. The two full pages of tables include some noneconomic statistics such as investor sentiment readings, the NYSE Data Bank, and the NYSE Members Report. All of these are more accurately defined as technical indicators that are related to the market, not to the economy.

It would be useful to readers if *Barron's* included a very brief description of the major tables and indicators, so the information could be more easily digested. *Barron's* provides explanatory footnotes and explanations for other sections of the paper, but the economic indicators are reported with little explanatory assistance. We might assume that only a few economists look at these reports, but if that is the case, why take up room in a paper for the less-interested typical investor? Because overall economic indicators are of questionable reliability and their application to investments is undefined, it is not clear why *Barron's* takes up the space with these data.

When it comes to a study of economic indicators, remember that it is all a matter of estimates and comparisons between today's indicator levels and an arbitrary starting point at some time in the past. Because it all involves estimation, the information is both unreliable and difficult to apply. How do you make an investment decision based on economic information? The answer is, you do not. These statistics can be useful in rounding out a comprehensive program of analysis, but they should not be used for making important decisions. Using any single indicator without confirmation from another is a mistake. The economy-wide economic indicators, by nature overly broad, are of no immediate or direct use in managing your individual portfolio.

INDEX

A–B

American Stock Exchange, 44–48
Analysis, 29, 33–35
Back-end load, 93
Barron's, 48–49, 75, 77, 81, 84, 85, 98–100, 104–7, 117–19, 126–28, 131–32, 135–37, 150–52, 159, 170, 175–78, 198–205
Bond
  agency, 80–82
  callable, 90
  convertible, 90
  corporate, 82–85
  descriptions, 71–72
  evaluation, 86–91
  listings, 75–86
  money market, 85–86
  municipal, 81
  ratings, 73, 83, 86–87
  scope, 72–73
  vocabulary, 74–75
Brokerage Web sites, 30–31

C

Charting, 161–63
Closed-end funds, 103–4
Coincident economic indicators, 196
Commodities futures, 129–39
Corporate reports, 180–82
Coupon rate, 74, 76

D

Day trading, 35–39
Decimalization, 41–43
Derivatives, 113, 140–44
Dividends, 173–77

Dividend yield, 60, 67–68
Dow Jones Industrial Averages, 146

E

Earnings per share, 63–64
Earnings reports, 167–73
Economic indicators
  coincident, 196
  lagging, 196–97
  leading, 194–96
  measurements, 203–4
Efficient Market Hypothesis, 33

F

Financial news, 21–24, 55, 70
Financial Times, 53–54
Financial Times Stock Exchange (FTSE), 53–54
Front-end load, 93
Fundamental indicators, 164–67, 182–88
Fundamental information, 28–29

I

Index options, 123–29
Interest rates, 198–99
Investor's Business Daily, 50–53, 75, 77, 80, 81, 83, 86, 100–103, 119–20, 122, 128–29, 132–33, 137–38, 152–53, 160, 172

L

Lagging economic indicators, 196–97

Leading economic indicators,
 194–96
LEAPS, 120–22
London Stock Exchange, 53–54
London Times, 53, 54

M

Management fees, 94
Marketing fees (12b-1), 93–94
Metals prices, 201–2
Money market funds, 104–5
Money supply, 198–99, 201
Mutual fund
    charges, 93–95
    closed-end, 103–4
    holdings, 92
    listings, 107–12
    money market, 104–5
    net asset value, 111
    no-load, 94–95
    open-end, 95–103

N

Nasdaq, 44–48, 52–53
Net asset value, 111
New York Stock Exchange, 43–53,
 56
News
    comparisons, 1–7, 70
    index reporting, 7–8
    online, 17–21, 29–30
    reporting, 13–15
    research, 25–27, 30–32
    sources, 29–30, 55
No-load funds, 94–95

O

Odd-lot trends, 155–57
Open-end funds, 95–103
Options
    index options, 123–29
    LEAPS, 120–22

listed, 114–20
trading symbols, 140–42

P

Par value, 74
Price-earnings ratio (PE), 60–61,
 154–55
Price trends, 157–59
Profit reporting, 9–13

R

Radio news, 190–91
Random Walk Hypothesis, 33
Real estate indicators, 204–5, 206
Redemption fees, 94
Research, 25–27
Rumor, 15–17

S

Standard and Poor's, 29, 73
Standard and Poor's 500, 146
Stock listings
    American Stock Exchange,
     44–48
    charting, 161–63
    decimalization, 41–43
    dividends, 173–77
    earnings, 167–73, 180–82
    international, 53–54
    interpretation, 57–70
    Nasdaq, 44–48, 52–53
    New York Stock Exchange,
     43–53, 56
    price trends, 157–59
    reporting, 41–43
    splits, 176–77
    volume trends, 159–61
STRIPS, 76–78

T

Technical indicators, 145–46
Television news, 189–90
Treasury securities, 72–73, 75–82

U–V

USA Today, 55–57, 97
Value Line, 29
Variable annuities, 106–7
Volume, 61–62
Volume trends, 159–61

W–Y

Wall Street Journal, The, 44–48, 50,
    75, 77–78, 80, 81, 83, 85, 96, 98,
    115–17, 121–25, 129–31, 147–49,
    158, 168, 174
Yield to maturity, 74–75, 86